THE PHILOSOPHY OF David Hume

Eighteen of the most important books on Hume's philosophy reprinted in twenty volumes

Edited by
Lewis White Beck, The University of Rochester

A GARLAND SERIES

Letters to a Philosophical Unbeliever

Part I

Joseph Priestley

Garland Publishing, Inc.
New York & London 1983

For a complete list of the titles in this series
see the final pages of this volume.

This facsimile has been made from a copy in
the Yale University library.

Library of Congress Cataloging in Publication Data
Priestley, Joseph, 1733–1804.
Letters to a philosophical unbeliever, part I.
(The Philosophy of David Hume)
Reprint. Originally published in v. 4 of: The theological and
miscellaneous works of Joseph Priestley. London : Printed by
G. Smallfield, 1817–1832.
1. God.   2. Hume, David, 1711–1776. Dialogues concerning
natural religion.   3. Natural theology—Early works to 1900.
4. Gibbon, Edward, 1737–1794. History of the decline and fall
of the Roman empire.   5. Rome—History—Empire, 30
B.C.–476 A.D.   6. Byzantine Empire—History.
I. Title.   II. Series.
BL205.P725   1983   210   82-48338
ISBN 0-8240-5415-6

Design by Jonathan Billing

The volumes in this series are printed on acid-free,
250-year-life paper.

Printed in the United States of America

THE

𝕿𝖍𝖊𝖔𝖑𝖔𝖌𝖎𝖈𝖆𝖑 𝖆𝖓𝖉 𝕸𝖎𝖘𝖈𝖊𝖑𝖑𝖆𝖓𝖊𝖔𝖚𝖘

WORKS,

&c.

OF

JOSEPH PRIESTLEY, LL. D. F. R. S. &c.

WITH

NOTES,

BY THE EDITOR.

VOLUME IV.

Containing

A FREE DISCUSSION BETWEEN DR. PRICE AND DR. PRIESTLEY;

LETTERS

TO REV. J. BERRINGTON, DR. KENRICK, MR. J. WHITEHEAD, DR. HORSLEY, REV. J. PALMER, AND JACOB BRYANT, ESQ.;

𝕮𝖔𝖑𝖑𝖎𝖓𝖘'𝖘 𝕴𝖓𝖖𝖚𝖎𝖗𝖞;

AND

LETTERS TO *A PHILOSOPHICAL UNBELIEVER,*
Part I. and II.

LETTERS

TO A

Philosophical Unbeliever.

PART I.

CONTAINING

An Examination of the principal Objections to the Doctrines of Natural Religion, and especially those contained in the Writings of Mr. Hume.

> Scilicet haud satis est rivos spectare fluentes—
> Fontem ipsum spectare juvat.
> ANTI-LUCRETIUS.

[1780.]

[*Re-printed from the Second Edition* 1787.]

THE PREFACE.

It will, I think, be acknowledged by all persons who are capable of reflection, and who *do* reflect, that in the whole compass of speculation, there are no questions more interesting to all men than those which are the subject of these *Letters*, viz. Whether the world we inhabit, and ourselves who inhabit it, had an intelligent and benevolent author, or no proper author at all? Whether our conduct be inspected, and we are under a righteous government, or under no government at all? And, lastly, whether we have something to hope and fear beyond the grave, or are at liberty to adopt the Epicurean maxim, *Let us eat and drink for to-morrow we die?* This may strike us more forcibly if we attend a little to the principles of human nature.

The great superiority of man over brutes consists in the greater *comprehensiveness of his mind*, by means of which he is, as it is commonly expressed, capable of *reflection*, but more accurately speaking, capable of contemplating, and, therefore, of enjoying the *past* and the *future,* as well as the *present.* And what is most extraordinary and interesting to us, this power, as far as appears, has no limits.

In infancy we feel nothing but what affects us for the moment, but *present feelings* bear a less and less proportion to the general mass of sensation, as it may be called, consisting of various elements, the greatest part of which are borrowed from the *past* and the *future;* so that, in our natural progress in intellectual improvement, all temporary affections, whether of a pleasurable or of a painful nature, will come at length to be wholly inconsiderable, and we shall have, in a greater degree than we can at present conceive, an equable enjoyment of the whole of what we *have been* and *have felt*, and also of what we have a confident *expectation of being*, and of feeling in future.

Our progress, however, in this intellectual improvement is capable of being accelerated or retarded, according as we accustom ourselves to reflection or live without it. For certainly, though, while we retain the faculties of memory and reasoning, we cannot whether we choose it or not, wholly exclude reflection on the past or anticipation of the future, (and, therefore, some kind of advance in intellectual improvement is unavoidable to all beings possessed of intellect,) yet it is in our power to exclude what is of great moment, viz. all that is *voluntary* in the business; so that being in a great measure deaf to what is behind, and blind to what is before, we may give ourselves up to mere sensual gratifications, and, consequently, no question concerning what is *past* or *future* may interest us. In this state of mind a man may think it absurd to trouble himself either about how he came into the world, or how he is to go out of it.

It would be too hasty, however, to assert, that it can only be in this very lowest state of intellect, a life of mere sensation or very imperfect reflection, that any person can be unconcerned about the belief of a God and the doctrines of natural religion. For a man may get above mere sensual indulgence, and give great scope to his intellectual faculties with respect to some objects, and be wholly inattentive to others. And it is in the power of little things, by wholly occupying the mind, not only to exclude the consideration of greater things, but even the idea of their being greater.

This, indeed, comes within the description of a kind of proper *insanity*, but then it may be justly asserted, that in a greater or less degree, all persons who do not prize every thing according to its real value, and regulate their pursuits accordingly, are insane; though, when the degree is small, it passes unnoticed, and when the consequences are inconsiderable, it is far from being offensive. Nay, in some cases, the world derives great and manifest advantage from a partial disorder, as it may be called, of this kind. For great excellence in particular arts and sciences, is perhaps seldom attained without it. Indeed, it cannot be expected that a man should greatly excel in some things, without neglecting, and consequently, undervaluing others.

We are shocked at a man's insanity only when it makes him inattentive to things that immediately concern him, as to the necessary means of his subsistence or support, so that he must perish without the care of others. But when the interest, though real, is *remote*, a man's inattention to it passes unnoticed. By this means it is that, without being surprised or shocked, we every day see thousands, who profess to believe in a future world, live and die without making any provision for it, though their conduct is much more inexcusable than that of the atheist who, not believing in futurity, minds only what is present.

But though the conduct of the atheist be consistent with itself, it must give concern to those who are not atheists, and who have a just sense of the importance of the belief of a God, of a providence and of a future state, to the present dignity and the future happiness of man.

An atheist may be a temperate, good-natured, honest, and in the common, and less extended sense of the word, a *virtuous* man; because if he be a man of good understanding, of naturally moderate passions, and have been properly educated, the influences to which he will have been exposed may be sufficient to *form* those valuable and amiable habits, and to *fix* him in them. But, notwithstanding this, an atheist has neither the *motive* nor the *means* of being what he might have been if he had not been an atheist.

An atheist cannot have that sense of *personal dignity* and *importance* that a theist has. For he who believes that he was introduced into life without any design, and is soon to be for ever excluded from life, cannot suppose that he has any very important part to act in life: and, therefore, he can have no motive to give much attention to his conduct in it. The past and the future being of less consequence to him, he will naturally endeavour to think about them as little as possible, and make the most of what is before him.

But the necessary consequence of this is the *debasement of his nature*, or a foregoing of the advantages that he might have derived from that power of comprehension, which will have full scope in the theist; the man who considers himself as a link in an immensely connected chain of being, as acting a part in a *drama*, which commenced from eternity, and extends to eternity; who considers that every gratification and every action, contributes to form a *character*, the importance of which to him is, literally speaking, infinite; who considers himself as standing in the nearest and most desirable relation to a Being of infinite power, wisdom and goodness; a Being who gives unremitted attention to him, who plans for him, and conducts him through this life, who does not lose sight of him even in the grave, and who will, in due time, raise him to a life, which, with respect both to gratifications and pursuits, will be of unspeakably more value to him than the present, and whose views, with respect to him and the universe, are boundless.

A man who really believes this, and who gives that *attention* to it which its great importance to him manifestly requires, must be *another kind of being* than an atheist, and certainly a being of unspeakably greater dignity and value. His *feelings* and his *conduct* cannot but be greatly superior.

This, however, from the nature of the thing, must depend upon the *attention* that a theist gives to his principles, and to the situation in which he believes himself to be placed. And therefore, it is very possible that a merely *nominal believer* in a God may be a *practical atheist*, and worse than a mere speculative one, living as *without God in the world*, entirely thoughtless of his being, perfections and providence. But still, nothing but *reflection* is wanting to reclaim such a person, and recover him to a proper dignity of sentiment, and a propriety of conduct; whereas, an atheist thus sunk has not the same *power of recovery*. He wants both the *disposition* and the necessary *means*. His mind is destitute of the *latent seeds* of future greatness.

If, according to the observation of Lord Bacon, it be *knowledge* that constitutes *power:* if it be our knowledge of the external world that gives us such extensive power over *it*, and adds to our happiness in it, knowledge so materially respecting ourselves, our general situation and conduct, must have great power over *ourselves*. It must, as it were, new make us, and give us sentiments and principles greatly superior to any that we could otherwise be possessed of, and add to our *happiness* as much as it does to our *dignity*.

PREFACE. 321

If, as Mr. Hume observes,* "the *good*, the *great*, the *sublime*, the *ravishing*, be found eminently in the genuine principles of theism," I need not say that there must be something *mean*, *abject* and *debasing*, in the principles of atheism. If, as he also says, (p. 116,) " a people entirely devoid of religion" are sure to be " but few degrees removed from brutes," they must be this, or something worse than this, who, having been acquainted with the principles of religion, have discarded them. The consistency of these sentiments with those advanced in other parts of Mr. Hume's writings, it is not my business to look to.

I shall think myself happy if, in these *Letters*, I have advanced any thing that may tend either to lessen the number of speculative atheists, or, which is no less wanting, convert nominal believers into practical ones. It is not, in general, *reason* and *argument*, but the pleasures and bustle of the world that prevent both ; and proper moderation in our desires and pursuits, accompanied with serious reflection, would be of the greatest use in both cases. I wish to give occasion, and to furnish the means for this cool recollection of ourselves.

It is the too eager pursuit of pleasure, wealth, ambition, and I may add of the arts, and even of science (theological science itself not wholly excepted) that is our snare. All these may equally *occupy the mind*, to the exclusion of the greater views that open to us as *men* and subjects of moral government, who are but in the infancy of an endless, and, therefore, an infinitely important existence. All these pursuits are equally capable of confining our attention to what is immediately before us, and of hiding from our view whatever in the past or the future, most nearly concerns us to attend to.

The great book of nature is always open before us, and our eyes are always open upon it, but we pass our time in a kind of *reverie*, or absence of thought, inattentive to the most obvious connexions and consequences of things. The same is the case with the book of revelation. But it is the former only that I have a view to in the present publication.

My design, however, is to proceed to consider the speculative difficulties which attend the doctrines of *revelation*, with philosophical and thinking persons in the present age, if the reception of this part shall give me sufficient encouragement to proceed farther. But if I succeed in this

---

* In his *Dissertation* on the Natural History of Religion, p. 114. (*P.*) 1757.

first part, I shall consider my great object as nearly attained; there being, as I have reason to think, many more atheists at present than mere unbelievers in revelation, especially out of England; and, for my part, I cannot help considering the difficulties that attend the proof of the Jewish and Christian revelations, as not greater than those which relate to the doctrines of natural religion.

Whenever, therefore, I shall hear of the conversion of a speculative atheist to *serious deism* (an event which has never yet come to my knowledge) I shall have little doubt of his soon becoming a serious Christian. As, on the other hand, the same turn of mind that makes a man an unbeliever in Christianity has, in fact, generally carried men on to a proper atheism. But, in other cases, this progress in speculation requires some degree of *attention* to the subject; for, with a total *listlessness and unconcern*, a man may rest *any where*. He may understand the first book of Euclid, and have no knowledge of the second, and therefore, no opinion about any of the propositions in it.

In both parts of this work it is my wish to speak to *the present state of things*, and to consider the difficulties that really press the most, without discussing every thing belonging to the subject; for which I must refer to more systematic writers, and for a short view of the whole chain of argument, with some original illustrations to my *Institutes of Natural and Revealed Religion*. (Vol. II. pp. 1—25.)

In some respects, I may, perhaps, flatter myself that I write with more advantage than any of those who have preceded me in the same argument, as I shall particularly endeavour to avail myself of the real service that infidelity has been of to Christianity, in freeing it from many things which, I believe, all who have formerly undertaken the defence of it have considered as belonging to it; when they have, in reality, been things quite foreign to it, and in some cases subversive of it. I shall hope, therefore, to exhibit a view of Christianity to which a *philosopher* cannot have so much to object, every thing that I shall contend for, appearing to me perfectly consonant to the principles of sound philosophy; and I shall use no other *modes of reasoning* than those that are universally adopted in similar cases, as I hope to make appear. Whether I succeed to my wish or not, I shall be *ingenuous*, and as impartial as I can. As to any bias that I may lie under, those who know me and my situation, are the best judges; it being impossible I should be aware of this myself. Whatever cause we ourselves wish well to, we necessarily imagine we have sufficient reason for so wishing.

I m far from meaning to hold myself forth as an oracle in this business; but I shall be really obliged to any person who shall propose to me any objection that he really thinks materially to affect the credibility of the Jewish or the Christian system: no objection so proposed to me shall pass unnoticed, whether I be able to give satisfaction with respect to it or not. If I myself feel the difficulty, I shall freely acknowledge it, and endeavour to estimate the force of it.

I, together with the persons to whom I am addressing myself, am a speculative inhabitant of the earth, actuated by the same passions, engaged in a variety of the same pursuits, and (as we have not yet made any discovery that will enable us to cure the disease of *old age*, and to prolong life *ad libitum*) I, together with them, am hastening to the grave; and, therefore, I am equally interested with them to find whether any thing awaits us after death, and, if any thing, what it is. This is, in its own nature, a more important object of inquiry than any thing that we have hitherto so laboriously investigated. It behoves us, therefore, to be cool and patient, attentive to every circumstance that can throw light upon the great question, and to give one another all the assistance we can with respect to it.

Truth, and the *laws of nature*, are our common object; but we are necessarily more *interested* in the investigation, in proportion to the *magnitude* of the object and the *concern* we have in it. In these questions, therefore, there is a concurrence of every thing that can render the investigation interesting to us; and as there is no interference of *particular interests* in the case, there is all the reason imaginable to lay aside every prejudice, to unite our labours, and give one another all the assistance in our power, either by *proposing difficulties* or *solving* them. Assistance, in either of these forms, I sincerely intreat, and shall be truly thankful for.

With respect to this publication, concerning *natural religion*, it may not be improper to observe, as I did in my *Institutes of Natural and Revealed Religion*, " that, in giving a delineation of natural religion, I shall deliver what I suppose *might* have been known concerning God, our duty, and our future expectations, by the light of nature, and not what was *actually* known of them by any of the human race; for these are very different things. Many things are in their own nature attainable, which, in fact, are never attained; so that though we find but little of the knowledge of God and of his providence, in many nations, which never enjoyed the light of revelation, it does not follow, that nature did not contain and teach those lessons, and that men had not the means of learning them, provided they had made the most of the light they had, and of the powers that were given them. I shall, therefore, include, under the head of *natural religion*, all that can be *demonstrated* or proved to be true, by natural reason, though it was never, in fact, discovered by it; and even though it be probable, that mankind would never have known it without the assistance of revelation." (Vol. II. p. 2.)

Mr. Hume acknowledges, that the hypothesis, which would most naturally occur to uninstructed mankind to account for appearances in the world, would be that of *a multiplicity of deities;* * and of what mankind, who have been, as far as appears, altogether, or nearly self-taught, in this respect, have been capable, in many hundred, and, in some cases, probably, thousands of years, we have evidence enough. The experiment, as we may call it, has been tried both among the civilized and the uncivilized of our race.

Nothing, therefore, that I have advanced in this work, can be at all understood to lessen the great value of revelation, even admitting, what is far from being probable, that, in some very distant age of the world, men might have attained to a full persuasion concerning all the great truths of religion, as the unity of God, the doctrine of a resurrection to immortal life, and a state of future retribution. What the most enlightened of our race had conjectured concerning these things, in fact, led them rather farther from the truth than nearer to it, and never made much impression on the generality of mankind.

Plain as the great argument contained in these *letters* is, viz. that which establishes the belief of *a God* and a *benevolent providence*, I have not been able to reply to the objections that have been started on the subject, in such a manner as that I can promise myself will be perfectly intelligible to *all* my readers. But, in general, those persons who cannot fully comprehend the answers, will not be able to see the force of the objections; and, therefore, if they have no doubts themselves, and have no occasion to make themselves so far masters of the argument as to

---

* Polytheism or idolatry was, and necessarily must have been, the first and most ancient religion of mankind." *Dissert.* S. i. p. 3.

enable them to satisfy the doubts of others, they may very well content themselves with entirely omitting, or giving but little attention to the third, fourth, twelfth, thirteenth and fourteenth letters.

I give this notice, lest persons not used to metaphysical speculations, looking into those particular letters, and finding unexpected difficulties in the subject of them, should hastily conclude, that the whole is a business of *subtle disputation*, with respect to which, they could never hope to attain to any satisfactory determination, and therefore, that they may as well leave it to be discussed by idle and speculative people, without concerning themselves about it. Whereas, nothing can be more momentous in itself or more important to be known and *attended to*, than the general doctrine of these letters; and it equally concerns the wise and the ignorant, men of speculation or men of business, those who are capable of the greatest refinement, and those who cannot refine at all. For how different soever our turns of thinking, or modes of life, may be, we are all equally subjects of God's moral government, if there be a God and a governor, and equally *heirs of immortality*, if there be any immortality for man.

Some may consider the critical review of Mr. Hume's metaphysical writings, in the last of these letters, as ungenerous, now that he is dead and unable to make any reply. But this circumstance makes no difference in his particular case, as it was a maxim with him (and perhaps one instance of the great *wisdom* that Dr. Smith* ascribes to him) to take no notice of any objections to his writings; † and he has left behind him a guardian of his reputation, of ability, in my opinion, fully equal to his own, and whose friendship for him cannot be questioned.

---

* In the conclusion of his letter to Mr. Strahan, annexed to Hume's *Life*.
† See his *Own Life*, 1777, p. 15, and Vol. III. p. 204.

LETTERS

TO A

PHILOSOPHICAL UNBELIEVER.

―――♦―――

LETTER I.

Of the NATURE *of* EVIDENCE.

DEAR SIR,*

I AM sorry to find that, in consequence of the books you have lately read, and of the company you have been obliged to keep, especially on your travels, you have found your mind unhinged with respect to the first principles of religion, natural as well as revealed. You wish me to attempt the solution of the difficulties you have proposed to me on those subjects; and I shall, without much reluctance, undertake to give you all the satisfaction that I am able.

You have not, that I know, any vicious bias to mislead you, by secretly inclining you to disbelieve a system which threatens vice with future punishment. And, though it is always flattering to a person of a speculative turn to be ranked with those whose mode of thinking is the most *fashionable*, being connected with ideas of liberality, courage, manliness, freedom from vulgar prejudices, &c. yet, as you have not particularly distinguished yourself in this line, either by writing, taking the lead in conversation, or in any other way, I flatter myself that your bias of this kind (though it will draw you more strongly than you can be aware of yourself) may not be too strong for rational evidence, or such as the nature of the thing admits of.

---

* It appears from an early part of the author's *Memoirs*, that he was hardly " reconciled to the idea of writing to a fictitious person on this occasion, though," as he justly adds, " nothing can be more innocent, or sometimes more proper." In another part of the *Memoirs*, he says of these *Letters*, " Having conversed so much with unbelievers, at home and abroad, I thought I should be able to combat their prejudices with advantage, and with this view I wrote," &c.

Otherwise, you are not so little read in the world, as not to have perceived, that there are many prejudices which no *evidence* can overcome. No person can possibly be sensible of this in himself, but we all see it in others; and we see that it extends to subjects of all kinds, theology, metaphysics, politics and common life. These prejudices arise from what are commonly called *false views of things*, or improper associations of ideas, which in the extreme become *delirium* or *madness*, and are conspicuous to every person, except to him who actually labours under this disorder of mind.

Now, as the causes of the wrong associations of ideas affect men of letters as well as other persons (though generally in a different way, and perhaps not, upon the whole, in the same degree), they may have the same bias to incredulity in some cases, that others have to credulity; and the same person, who is the most unreasonably incredulous in some things, may be as unreasonably credulous, and even superstitious, in others; so little ought we to take it for granted, that a man who thinks rationally on some subjects will do so uniformly, and may be confided in as a safe guide in all. This, however, is agreeable to other analogies; as, for instance, with respect to courage; for the extreme of bravery in some respects is often found united with the extreme of cowardice in others.

You know a friend of ours, by no means deficient in point of general understanding, who to the fashionable infidelity adds the fashionable follies of the age. Though he believes nothing of *invisible powers* of any kind, he has a predilection for a certain class of numbers in the lottery, and, when he is eagerly engaged in gaming, must throw his dice in particular, and what we think whimsical, circumstances. Now, what is this better than *whistling for a wind* (which, however, we find many sensible sailors continue to practise), the *Roman auguries*, or the weakest of the Popish superstitions?

The fact is, that in some manner, which perhaps neither himself nor any other person can explain, he has connected in his mind the idea of some peculiar circumstances with that of a successful throw, and the idea of other peculiar circumstances with that of an unsuccessful one, just as we happen to connect in our minds the ideas of *darkness* and of *apparitions*; which association, when it is once formed, often affects the mind more or less through life, and long after all belief in apparitions is given up, and even ridiculed.

I might enforce this observation, which is far from being

foreign to our present purpose, by reminding you, that there are both able and upright men on both sides of what we think the clearest of all questions, in morals, theology and politics. How often have you expressed your astonishment, that any person should hold the doctrine that you reprobate concerning the *Middlesex election*, and the *taxation of America*, and yet think himself the friend of liberty, and the enemy of all oppression and tyranny.

Had not mortality come in aid of the demonstrations on which the Newtonian system of the universe is founded, it is not certain that it would even yet have supplanted the Aristotelian, or Cartesian system, ill-founded as they were. But the old and incorrigibly bigoted abettors of former hypotheses leaving the stage, reason had a better chance with the younger, and the less biassed.

When you reflect on these, and many other facts of the same nature, you will not wonder much, that so many sensible men of your acquaintance, and men of an ingenuous and candid disposition in other respects, struck with the glaring absurdities and mischiefs of superstition, should think it wise and right to take refuge in irreligion, and, not seeing where they can consistently stop, even disclaim the belief of a God. Nor do I wonder that, being men of ingenuity, their reasonings on these subjects should have staggered you. All this may be the case, and yet those reasonings be altogether inconclusive.

As you profess you have no objection to my considering you as ignorant as I please in every thing relating to this subject, I shall, in order to lay the surest foundation of a truly rational faith, take the liberty to begin with explaining what appears to me to be the natural ground of *evidence*, or of the *assent* that we give to propositions of all kinds, that we may see afterwards how far it may be applied to the subject of religion.

Now every *proposition*, or every thing to which we give our assent, or dissent, consists ultimately of two terms, one of which is affirmed of the other; as that *twice two is four*, the *three angles of every right-lined triangle are equal to two right angles; man is mortal, air is elastic*, &c. And the ground of our affirming one of these ideas of the other is either that, when they are considered, they appear to be in fact, the same idea, or perfectly to coincide; or else that the one is constantly observed to accompany the other. Thus the reason why I affirm that *twice two is four*, is, that the idea annexed to the term *twice two*, coincides with the idea annexed to the term *four;* so does the idea of the quantity annexed to the *three angles of a right-lined triangle* with that of *two right angles.* But the reason why I affirm that *man is mortal* is of a different nature, and is founded on the observation that all men are found to be so; and I say that *air is elastic,* because every substance that bears that denomination is found to restore itself to its former dimensions, or nearly so, after having been compressed.

Propositions of the former kind, if they be true at all, are universally and necessarily so, and the evidence for them is called *demonstration.* Of this kind are the indisputable propositions in geometry and algebra. But propositions of the latter kind are always liable to be corrected and modified by subsequent and more exact observations; because it is not by comparing our own ideas only that we come to the knowledge of their truth, and later observations may correct what was defective in former ones.

There are, however, propositions of the former kind, the proof of which is not strictly demonstrative, because the evidence of it does not arise from the comparison of our ideas, but from the testimony of others, the validity of which rests ultimately on the association of ideas; human testimony in certain circumstances not having been found to deceive us. Of this kind is the proposition *Alexander conquered Darius.* For the proof of it is complete, when it appears that the person distinguished by the name of Alexander, is the same with him that conquered Darius. But since the evidence of this can never be made out by any operations on my own ideas, I have recourse to the testimony of others; and I believe the proposition to be true, because I have all the reason I can have, to think that a history so authenticated as that of Alexander and Darius may be depended on.

Now, it is not pretended, that the evidence of the propositions in natural or revealed religion is always of the former of these two kinds, but generally of the latter, or that which depends on the association of ideas; and in revealed religion, the evidence chiefly arises from testimony, but such testimony as has never yet been found to deceive us. I do not therefore say, that I can properly *demonstrate* all the principles of either; but I presume that, if any person's mind be truly unprejudiced, I shall be able to lay before him such evidence of both, as will determine his assent; and, in some of the cases, his *persuasion* shall hardly be distinguishable, with respect to its *strength*, from that which arises from a demonstration properly so called, the difference being, as mathematicians say, less than any assignable quantity. For no person, I presume, has, in fact, any more doubt either of there having been such a person as Alexander, or of his having conquered Darius, than he has of any proposition whatever. And yet sufficient and plenary as this evidence appears to me, it may fall far short of producing conviction in the minds of all; for, in some cases, we have seen that demonstration itself will not do this.

I am, &c.

LETTER II.

Of the direct Evidence for the Belief of a GOD.

DEAR SIR,

HAVING premised the observations contained in the preceding letter on the nature of evidence, I proceed to observe, that no person can live long in the world without knowing that men make *chairs* and *tables*, build *houses* and write *books*, and that chairs, tables, houses, or books, are not made without men. This constant and indisputable observation lays the foundation for such an association of the ideas of chairs, tables, houses and books, with that of *men* as the makers of them, that whenever we see a chair, a table, a house, or a book, we entertain no doubt but, though we did not see *when* or *how* they were made, and nobody gives us any information on the subject, yet that some man or other *did* make them. No man can ever suppose that a chair, a table, a house, or a book, was either the production of any tree, or came into being of itself. Nothing, in the course of his own experience or that of others, can lead him to imagine any such thing.

He afterwards sees birds build nests, spiders make webs, bees make honeycombs, &c. and accordingly he, as before, associates in his mind the ideas of all these things with that of the animals that made them; and therefore he concludes, when he sees a *honeycomb*, for instance, that *bees* have been at work upon it.

Finding, however, that some animals can, to a certain degree, imitate the works of others, and man those of most of them, he sees reason to limit his former conclusion, that such a particular animal, and no other, must necessarily have produced them, but (generalizing his ideas, from observing something of the same nature in whatever can produce the same thing, and calling it *similar power*) he says, that some being, of *sufficient powers*, has produced it.

Advancing, as he necessarily must, in the habit of generalizing his ideas, he calls chairs, tables, nests, webs, &c. by the general term *effects*, and men, animals, &c. that produce them, by the term *causes;* and expressing the result of all his observations, he concludes universally, that *all effects have their adequate causes.* For he sees nothing come into being, in any other way.

He likewise sees one plant proceed from another, and one animal from another, by natural vegetation, or generation, and therefore he concludes that every plant and every animal had its proper parent. But the parent plant, or parent animal, does not bear the same relation to its offspring that men do to chairs, books, &c. because they have no *design* in producing them, and no *comprehension* of the nature or use of what they produce. There is, however, some analogy in the two cases; and therefore the parent plant, or parent animal, is still termed a *cause*, though in a less proper sense of the word. However, admitting these to be called causes, it is still universally true, that *nothing begins to exist without a cause.* To this rule we see no exception whatever, and therefore cannot possibly entertain a doubt with respect to it.

Again, wherever there are *proper causes*, as of *men* with respect to *chairs, books*, &c. we cannot but be sensible that these causes must be capable of comprehending the nature and uses of those productions of which they are the causes, and *so far* as they are the causes of them. A carpenter may know nothing of the texture of the wood on which he works, or the cause of its colour, &c. for with respect to *them* he is no cause; but being the proper cause of the conversion of the wood into a chair, or table, he (or the person who employed him, or who first constructed these things, &c.) must have had an adequate idea of their nature and uses.

Observations of this kind extending themselves every day, it necessarily becomes a maxim with us, that wherever there is a fitness or correspondence of one thing to another, there must have been a cause capable of comprehending, and of designing that fitness. The first model of a windmill could not have been made by an idiot. Of such conclusions as these we have so full a persuasion, from constant experience and observation, that no man, let him pretend what he will, can entertain a serious doubt about the matter. The experience and observations of all men, without exception, are so much alike, that such associations of ideas as these must necessarily have been formed in all their minds, so that there is no possible cause of any difference of opinion on the subject.

Thus far we seem to tread upon firm ground, and every human being, I doubt not, will go along with me. And if they go thus far, I do not see how they can help going one step farther, and acknowledge, that if a *table* or a *chair* must have had a designing cause capable of comprehending their nature and uses, the *wood*, or the *tree*, of which the table was made, and also the *man* that constructed it, must likewise have had a designing cause, and a cause or author capable of comprehending all the powers and properties of which they are possessed, and therefore of an understanding greatly superior to that of any man, who is very far, indeed, from comprehending his own frame; being obliged to study it, and make discoveries concerning it, by degrees, as he does with respect to other things most foreign to himself, in the general system of nature. And of the nature of the immediate *perceptive power* itself, it is no more possible that he should have any idea, than that an eye should see itself.

This reasoning, wherever it may lead us, I do not see how we can possibly refuse to follow, because it is exactly the same that we set out with, arising from our own *immediate experience*. No person will say that one table might make another, or that one man might make another. Nothing that man does approaches to it. And if no man now living could do this, neither could any man's father, or most remote ancestor; because we see no such difference in any beings of the same species. Though, therefore, it should even be allowed, that *the species* had no beginning, it would not follow that it could be *the cause of itself*, or that it had *no cause;* for the idea of a cause of any thing implies not only something prior to itself, or at least contemporary with itself, but something capable at least of comprehending what it produces; and our going back ever so far in the generations of men or animals, brings us no nearer to the least degree of satisfaction on the subject. After thinking in this train ever so long, we find we might just as well suppose that any individual man now living was the first, and without cause, as either any of his ancestors, or *the species itself.* For, that there is such a contrivance in the structure of a man's body, and especially something so wonderful in the faculties of his mind, as exceeds the comprehension of *man*, cannot be denied.

For the same reason that the human species must have had a designing cause, all the species of brute animals, and the *world* to which they belong, and with which they make but *one system*, and indeed all the *visible universe* (which, as far as we can judge, bears all the marks of being *one work*) must have had a cause or author, possessed of what we may justly call *infinite power and intelligence*. For, in our endeavours to form an idea of something actually infinite, we shall fall greatly short of an idea of such intelligence as must belong to the author of the system.

It follows, therefore, from the most irresistible evidence, that the world must have had a designing cause, distinct from, and superior to itself. This conclusion follows from the strongest analogies possible. It rests on our own constant experience, and we may just as well say, that a *table* had not a designing cause, or no cause distinct from itself, as that the *world*, or the *universe*, considered as one system, had none. This necessary cause we call *God*, whatever other attributes he be possessed of.

Whatever difficulties we may meet with as we proceed, *so far* we must go, if we advance even the first step; and not to admit the first step, that is, not to admit that such a thing as a *table* had a prior and superior cause, would be universally judged to proceed from some very uncommon disorder in the mental faculties, and to be incompatible with a sound state of mind.

I shall, in my next, proceed to consider the difficulties that have been started on this subject by metaphysical writers; and whether I be able to do it to your satisfaction or not, I will, at least, do it with all possible fairness. In the mean time,

I am, &c.

LETTER III.

Objections *considered*.

Dear Sir,

Hitherto we have met with nothing that deserves to be called *a difficulty* in the proof of the being of a God; and if nothing more could be advanced on the subject, it would, I think, justify us in refusing to attend to any thing that could be said by way of *objection;* because so far we have what is fully equivalent to a *demonstration* of the existence of a primary, intelligent cause. I shall now, however, proceed to the consideration of the principal difficulties that have been started on the subject.

The first in importance is, that, for the same reason that the universe requires an intelligent cause, that intelligent cause must require a superior intelligent cause, and so on *ad infinitum,* which is manifestly absurd. We may just as well, therefore, it is alleged, acquiesce in saying, in the first instance, that the universe had no cause, as proceed to say that the cause of the universe had none.

I answer, that to acquiesce in saying that the universe had no cause is, for the reasons that have been given already, absolutely *impossible,* whatever be the consequence. If, therefore, there be ever so little less difficulty on the other side of the dilemma, viz. that the cause of the universe had no cause, it is to that that we must incline.

Let us see then whether there be any other supposition, which, though it be a *difficulty,* or *incomprehensible* by us, does not directly contradict our experience, or whether by some independent argument it may not be proved, that, incomprehensible as it is, there *must* have been an *uncaused intelligent Being.*

Both these things have, in fact, been done before; but I shall here repeat them with illustrations, adapted to this particular difficulty, and, in order to this, I shall resume the argument in the following different manner.

Something must have existed from all eternity, for otherwise nothing could have existed at present. This is too evident to need illustration. But this *original being,* as we may call it, could not have been such a thing as a table, an animal, or a man, or any being *incapable of comprehending itself,* for such a one would require a prior, or superior author. The original being, therefore, must have had this prerogative as well as have been necessarily *uncaused.*

It is not improper to call a being, incapable of comprehending itself, *finite,* and a being, originally and necessarily capable of it, *infinite,* for we can have no idea of any bounds to such knowledge or power; and, using the words in this sense, we may, perhaps, be authorized to say, that, though a finite being must have a cause, an infinite one does not require it. Though it is acknowledged, that these conclusions are above our comprehension, they are such as, by the plainest and the most cogent train of reasoning, we have been *compelled* into, and therefore, though, on account of the finiteness of our understanding, it may be said to be *above* our reason to comprehend *how* this original being, and the cause of all other beings, should be himself uncaused, it is a conclusion by no means properly *contrary* to reason. Indeed, what the universally established mode of reasoning, founded on our own immediate experience, obliges us to conclude, can never be said to be contrary to reason, how *incomprehensible* soever it may be by our reason.

That there actually is an *uncaused intelligent Being*, is a necessary conclusion from what does actually exist; for a series of finite causes cannot possibly be carried back *ad infinitum*, each being supposed capable of comprehending its own effects, but not itself. Since, therefore, an universe, bearing innumerable marks of most exquisite design, *does exist*, and it would be absurd to go back through an infinite succession of finite causes, we *must* at last acquiesce in the idea of an uncaused intelligent cause of this universe, and of all the intermediate finite causes, be they ever so many.

On this side there is only a *difficulty of conceiving*, but nothing *contrary to our experience*, and there is plainly no other choice left us. Our experience relates only to such things as are incapable of comprehending themselves, or finite, and therefore require a cause. Consequently, though this experience furnishes a sufficient analogy for judging concerning all other things which have the *same property*, it by no means furnishes any analogy by which to judge concerning what is totally different from any thing to which our experience extends; things not finite, but infinite, not destitute of original self-comprehension, but possessed of it. Here is so great a difference, that, as the one must necessarily be *caused*, the other may be necessarily *uncaused*.

Though nothing can properly help our conception in a case so much above the reach of our faculties, it may not be amiss to have recourse to any thing in the least degree similar, though equally incomprehensible, as it may make it easier to us to acquiesce in our necessary want of comprehension on the subject. Now, in some respects, the idea of *space*, though not intelligent, and therefore incapable of self-comprehension, and no cause of any thing, is similar to that of the intelligent cause of all things, in that it is necessarily *infinite* and *uncaused*. For the ideas of the creation, or of the annihilation of space, are equally inadmissible. Though we may, in our imagination, exclude from existence every thing else, still the idea of *space* will remain. We cannot, even in idea, suppose it not to *have been*, not to be *infinite*, or not to be *uncaused*. Now it may be, in fact, as impossible that an *intelligent infinite Being* should not exist, as that *infinite space* should not exist, though we are necessarily incapable of perceiving that it *must* be so.

If it be said that space is properly nothing at all, I answer, that space has real properties, as cannot be denied, and I know of no other definition of a *substance* than that which has properties. Take away all the properties of *any thing*, and nothing will be left; just so also, and no otherwise, nothing will be left of *space* when the properties of length, breadth and depth, are supposed to be taken away.

Secondly, it may be said, that *a whole* may have properties which the parts have not, as a sound may proceed from the vibration of a string, the component particles of which could not produce any, or as the faculty of thinking may be the result of a certain arrangement of the parts of the brain, which separately have no thought. I answer, that it cannot but be that every *whole* must have some properties which do not belong to the *separate parts*, but still, if all the separate parts require a cause, the whole must; and whatever peculiar powers belong to a whole, as such, they must be such as necessarily result from the arrangement of the parts and the combination of their powers. But no combination or arrangement whatever of *caused beings* can constitute an *uncaused* one. This affects us like a manifest contradiction.

To say, that the whole universe may have no cause, when it is acknowledged that each of its parts, separately taken, must have had one, would be the same thing as saying that *a house* may have had no maker, though the walls, the roof, the windows, the doors, and all the parts of which it consists, must have had one. Such a conclusion, with respect to a house, or the universe, would equally contradict our *constant experience*, and what we may call our *common sense*.

With respect to *thinking*, we only do not see *how* it results from the arrangement of matter, when facts prove that it *does* result from it, the properties of *thinking* and *materiality* being only *different*, not *contrary*; whereas, *caused* and *uncaused* are the direct reverse of each other.

Supposing, however, that intelligence *could* result from the present arrangement of such bodies as the sun, the earth, and the other planets, &c. (which, however, is so unlike the uniform composition of a *brain*, that the argument from analogy entirely fails) so that all that is *intellectual* in the universe should be the necessary result of what is not intellectual in it, and, consequently, there should be what has sometimes been called *a soul of the universe*, the hypothesis is, in fact, that of a deity, though we ourselves should enter into the composition of it, and there would be a real foundation for religion. But our imagination revolts at the idea, and we are compelled, as the easiest solution of the phenomena, to acquiesce in the belief of an intelligent uncaused Being, entirely distinct from the universe of which he is the author.

Thirdly, it will be said, that, as all the intelligence that we are acquainted with resides in the brains of men and animals, the Deity, if he be a being distinct from the universe, and intelligent, must, whatever be his form, have in him something resembling the structure of the brain.

I answer, that the preceding train of reasoning proves the contrary. An uncaused intelligent author of nature, and one that is distinct from it, there must be. This Being, however, is not the object of our senses. Therefore the seat of intelligence, though it be something visible and tangible in us, is not *necessarily* and *universally* so.

Besides, it only follows from the Deity and the human brain being both intelligent, that they must have this in common, and something (if any such thing there be) on which that property depends; but this may not be any thing necessarily connected with what is visible or tangible, or the object of any of our senses. Many things have common properties that are very dissimilar in other respects. If we had known nothing *elastic* besides *steel*, we might have concluded that nothing was elastic but steel, or something equally solid and hard; and yet we find elasticity belong to so rare a substance as *air*, and altogether unlike steel in every other respect. The divine mind, therefore, may be intelligent, in common with the mind of man, and yet not have the visible and tangible properties, or any thing of the *consistence* of the brain.

There are many *powers* in nature, even those by which bodies are acted upon, where nothing is visible; as the power of *gravitation*, and of *repulsion* at a distance from the visible surfaces of bodies. There are even such powers in places occupied by other bodies. Both gravitation and magnetism act through substances interposed between the bodies possessed of them, and those on which they act.

The Divine power, therefore, may penetrate, and fill all space, occupied or unoccupied by other substances, and yet be itself the object of none of our senses. And what do we mean by *substance*, but that in which we suppose powers to reside; so that wherever powers can exist, what we call the substance cannot be excluded, unless we suppose beings to act where they are not.

Fourthly. It was said by the atheists among the ancients, that the universe might have been formed by the *fortuitous concourse of atoms*, which had been in motion from all eternity, and therefore must, they say, have been in all possible situations.

But, besides many other improbabilities, which may make it doubtful whether any person was ever really satisfied with the hypothesis, those who advanced it were not philosophers enough to know what *atoms* are. If we have any ideas to words, atoms must mean *solid particles of matter*, that is, masses of matter; which, however small, are perfectly *compact*, and therefore consist of parts that have strong powers of *attraction*. But what reason have we, from experience, to suppose it possible, that these small masses of matter could have those powers without communication *ab extra* ?

In what respects could those atoms differ from pieces of wood, stone, or metal, at present; and is a piece of wood, stone, or metal, capable even of comprehending, much less of communicating its own powers, any more than a magnet? As well, therefore, might a magnet have been originally existent, as any coherent atom, or an atom possessed of the most simple powers whatever. In fact, we may just as well suppose a *man* to have been that originally existent being, as either of them.

Besides, admitting the existence of these original atoms, can we suppose them to have been moved any otherwise than as such bodies are moved at present, that is, by an external force? It is directly repugnant to all our experience to suppose any such thing; and could they be arranged in a manner expressive of the most exquisite design, without a mover possessed of competent intelligence?

Thus far, I flatter myself, I have advanced on sufficiently solid ground, in proving that there must have been an originally intelligent cause of the universe, distinct from the universe itself; or that *there is a God*. In proceeding farther I cannot promise to be always quite so clear, but I will promise to be *ingenuous*, pursuing such analogies as I am able to find, and no farther than they will naturally lead me.

Whether what I have already advanced will appear as satisfactory to you as it does to me, I cannot tell. If your mind be as unbiassed, as I am willing to hope it is, I think it must make some impression; for there is a strong natural evidence in favour of the belief of a God, and only something *incomprehensible* to us, but by no means contrary to evidence or reason, against it. And there is something so pleasing in the idea of a Supreme *Author*, and consequently, as I shall shew, of a Supreme *Governor* of the world, to virtuous and ingenuous minds, infinitely preferable to the idea of *a blind fate* and a *fatherless deserted world*, that if the mind was only *in equilibrio* with respect to the argument, it would, in fact, be determined by this bias. A truly ingenuous mind, therefore, will not only decide in favour of the belief of a God, but will so decide with joy.

I am, &c.

LETTER IV.

Of the necessary Attributes of the original Cause of all Things.

DEAR SIR,

IN the preceding letters I hope I have removed your greatest difficulties with respect to the belief of an *original intelligent cause of the universe;* having proved that, how incomprehensible soever such a Being may be to us, yet that such a Being must necessarily exist. My argument in short was this: There are in the universe innumerable and most evident marks of *design*, and it is directly contrary to all our observation and experience, to suppose that it should have come into being without a cause adequate to it, with respect both to power and intelligence. A Being, therefore, possessed of such power and intelligence, *must* exist. If this Being, the immediate maker of the universe, has not existed from all eternity, he must have derived his being and powers from one who has; and this *originally existent and intelligent Being*, which the actual existence of the universe compels us to come to at last, is the Being that we call *God*.

It is of no avail to say, that we have no *conception* concerning the original existence of such a Being, for our having *no idea at all* of any thing, implies no impossibility or contradiction whatever. This is mere *ignorance*, and an ignorance which, circumstanced as we are, we can never overcome; and the *actual phenomena* cannot be accounted for without the supposition of such a Being. Incomprehensible as it may be in ever so many respects, it is an hypothesis that is absolutely necessary to account for evident *facts*. We may, therefore, give what scope we will to our astonishment and admiration, yet *believe* (if we be guided by demonstrative evidence) we *must*. And it is a belief mixed with joy as well as with wonder. Let us now consider what may be either necessarily inferred, or is with the greatest probability implied, in the idea of this *original cause of all things*.

The first observation I would make is, that this Being must be what we term *infinite*, that is, since he is intelligent, there can be no bounds to his intelligence, or he must know all that is capable of being known; and since he is powerful (his works corresponding to what we call effects of power), his power must be infinite, or capable of producing whatever is possible in itself.

Since the reason why we cannot help concluding that a man, or any other being that we are acquainted with, could not be this originally existent Being, is the *limitation* of his knowledge and power (not being capable even of comprehending any thing equal to himself), and since this must have been the case with respect to any other being, how great soever, who had not this self-comprehension, the originally existing Being must necessarily have this power. A Being perfectly comprehending himself and every thing else, cannot have knowledge less than what may, in one sense at least, be termed infinite, for it comprehends *every thing* that exists. Admitting this, we cannot suppose that it does not likewise extend to every thing that *necessarily follows* from all that actually exists; and after this, we shall not know how to suppose that he should not be able to know what would be the result of any *possible* existence, for we cannot think this to be more difficult than the former.

Besides, in pursuance, in some measure, of this argument, we cannot help concluding, that a power capable of producing all that actually exists (so immense and wonderful is what is known of the system of the universe!) must be equal to any effect that is *possible in itself*. At least, if this inference be not strictly *necessary*, yet, having been compelled to admit the existence of a power so far exceeding all that we can comprehend, and all that we can imagine, when we even strain our conceptions to form an idea of infinite, we can see no reason why it should not be actually and strictly so.

Nay, having arrived at the knowledge of a Being who must have the power of self-comprehension, and also that of producing all that exists, we seem to require some external positive *cause of limitation* to his knowledge and power; which external positive cause we look for in vain. We therefore cannot feel the least reluctance in acquiescing in the belief that the original author of all things is infinite in knowledge and power. Having proved him to be capable of knowing and doing *so much*, we should, from a natural analogy, even revolt at the idea of his not being able to know and to do even *more*, if more were possible. This persuasion we arrive at by pursuing the most natural train of reasoning, and the most obvious deductions from the premises before us; so that any other inferences would be *unnatural*. We need not scruple, therefore, to consider it as an undoubted truth, however exceeding our comprehension, and therefore our power of *proper demonstration*, that God, the originally existing being, or the first cause of all things, is a being of strictly infinite power and knowledge.

Secondly. He must be *omnipresent*, or occupy all space, though this attribute is equally incomprehensible by us with the infinite extent of his power or knowledge.

That God must be present to all his works is a necessary conclusion; while we all admit that no power can act but where it is. Besides, existing, as he does, without any foreign cause, by what we call (though inaccurately, as all our language on this subject must be) *a natural necessity*, there can be no reason why he should exist in one place and not in another. He must, therefore, exist equally in all places, even through the boundless extent of infinite space, an idea just as incomprehensible as his necessary existence, but not more so. After this, the probability will be, that his *works*, as well as *himself*, occupy the whole extent of space, infinite as it must necessarily be, and that as *he* could have had no beginning, so neither had his works.

Having been obliged to admit so much that is altogether incomprehensible by us, it is by an easy chain of consequences that we come to these farther conclusions, which are not more incomprehensible than the former. Nay, if the universe had bounds, we should, if we reflect on the subject, be apt to wonder at those bounds, as much as we should wonder at any limitation to the knowledge of a Being who has the inconceivable power of self-comprehension, or at the limitation of his power who has produced the universe.

Again, that a Being, infinitely intelligent and infinitely powerful, should remain inactive a whole eternity, which must have been the case if the creation had any beginning at all, is also an idea that we can never reconcile ourselves to. An eternal creation, being the act of an eternal Being, is not at all more incomprehensible than the eternal existence of that Being himself. Both are incomprehensible, but the one is the most natural consequence of the other. In fact, there is no greater objection to the supposition of the *creation* having been eternal, than to *duration itself* having been eternal; for there cannot be any assignable or imaginable period in duration, in which the creation might not have taken place.*

Thirdly. That this infinite Being, who has existed without change, must continue to exist without change, to eternity, is likewise a conclusion that we cannot help drawing, though, the subject being incomprehensible, we may not be able to complete the demonstration. It is, however, little, if at all, short of the force of a demonstration, that the same *natural necessity* by which he always has existed, must, of course, prevent any change whatever. Besides, if any cause of change had existed, it must have operated in a whole eternity that is already past. We should also naturally conclude that, as no being could *make* himself (since that would imply that he existed and did not exist at the same time), so neither can any being *unmake*, or materially change, at least not *annihilate* himself; and, being omnipotent, no other being, especially none that he himself has produced (and in reality there cannot be any other), can be supposed capable of producing any change in him. Whatever, therefore, the Supreme Being is, and always has been, he ever must be.

Fourthly. There cannot be more than *one* such being as this. Though this proposition may not be strictly demonstrable by us, it is a supposition more natural than any other, and it perfectly harmonizes with what has been strictly proved and deduced already. Nay, there seems to be something hardly distinguishable from a contradiction in the supposition of there being *two infinite beings of the same kind*, since, in idea, they would perfectly *coincide*. We clearly perceive

---

* This opinion of the infinity and eternity of the works of an infinite and eternal Deity, though it seems to me to be the most probable, is by no means a necessary part of the system of natural religion. The belief of the existence of a God, and of a providence, may very well be held without it. (*P.*) See p. 148, and Vol. II. p. 5.

that there cannot be two *infinite spaces;* and since the analogy between this infinite unintelligent being, as we may call it, and the infinite intelligent one, has been seen to be pretty remarkable in one instance, it may be equally strict here; so that, were our faculties equal to the subject, and had we proper *data*, I think we should expect to perceive, that there could no more be two infinite, intelligent and omnipresent Beings, than there can be two infinite spaces.

Indeed their being *numerically two* would, in some measure, limit one another; so that, by the reasoning we have hitherto followed, neither of them could be the originally existent Being. Supposing them to be equally omnipotent, and that one of them should intend to do, and the other to undo, the same thing, their power would be equally balanced; and if their intentions always coincided, and they equally filled all space, they would be as much, and to all intents and purposes, *one and the same being*, as the coincidence of two infinite spaces would make but one infinite space.

I appeal to yourself, whether, after having admitted what the *actual phenomena* of nature compel us to admit, we could, without a real difficulty, and a manifest incongruity in our mode of reasoning, stop in any part of the progress through which I have now led you, whether every succeeding step has been a strictly necessary consequence of the preceding or not. Nay, the inferences have been so natural, that we cannot help suspecting that it is owing to the imperfection of our faculties, and our necessarily imperfect knowledge of the subject, that we do not *see* the inferences to be perfectly strict and conclusive.

We can hardly doubt but that a Being of infinite knowledge must clearly comprehend them all; that such a Being must be able to perceive both that, independently of every thing else actually existing, *he himself* could not but have existed; that he could not but have had *infinite knowledge and power;* that he could not have been excluded from any part of even infinite space; that he could not but have acted from all eternity; that he could not be subject to any change, and that there could not be any other being equal or comparable to himself, or that should not be dependent upon himself. We do not see the necessary connexion of all these properties, and therefore we cannot see *how* any other being can; but the case is such, that we cannot help suspecting that it is owing to our imperfection that we are not able to do it.

If you say that I have bewildered and confounded you

with these speculations, you must, however, acknowledge, that it has been in consequence of following the best lights the subject could afford us; and that to have come to any other conclusions, we must, in all cases, have taken a less probability instead of a greater, and something less instead of something more consonant to what we were, from the first, compelled by the plainest phenomena, to admit.

You will please, however, to observe that, in all this, I do not pretend to prove *a priori* that, without any regard to the supposition of an external world, there must have been what may be called a *self-existent Being;* but only that, having first proved, from the phenomena of nature, that there must have been an eternally existing intelligent Being, we cannot help concluding (at least according to the strongest probabilities) that, in consequence of being *originally existing*, and the intelligent cause of all things, he must be infinitely knowing and powerful, fill infinite space, and have no equal.

I am, &c.

LETTER V.

The Evidence for the GENERAL BENEVOLENCE *of the Deity.*

DEAR SIR,

I FLATTER myself that, in the preceding letters, I have removed, or at least have lessened, your difficulties relating to the arguments for the being and primary attributes of the Deity. It is true that I have led you into the region of *infinites* and *incomprehensibles*, but then *reason* herself conducted us thither, and we did not lose sight of her while we were there. Among infinites there are analogies peculiar to themselves, and those who cannot form an adequate idea of any thing infinite may yet judge of those *analogies*, as well as of those of finites. Infinites frequently occur in geometrical and algebraical investigations, and yet the most clear and undeniable consequences may be drawn from them.

The phenomena of nature prove that there must have been some *originally existent being*, and of such a nature, that it could not derive its existence and powers from any thing prior to it. Consequently, it could not be any thing of a finite nature, such as plants or animals, or any thing that we see here; for these, not being able even to comprehend their own constitution, must necessarily have derived it from some being of superior knowledge and power; and the idea of the degree of knowledge and power requisite to form such a system as this, of which we are a part, cannot be distinguished from that of *infinite*. Indeed, had it been, in any respect, finite, it would only have been in the condition of a plant, or an animal, of a more perfect kind, and therefore, like them, would have required a superior cause. The evident probability therefore is, that the original intelligent cause of all things, and who must necessarily have been *uncaused*, is, in the strictest sense of the word, *infinite* in knowledge and power; as, for reasons that have been given, he must likewise be infinite in duration and extension, or commensurate with all time and all space. And though we are utterly at a loss to conceive *how* so great a being as this should himself require no cause, it is even demonstrable both that such a being *doth* exist, and that he *could not* have any cause, and therefore we *must* acquiesce in our inability of having any ideas on the subject.

This case is, however, evidently different from that of all finite beings, all of which necessarily require a cause; and, though we cannot conceive it, the reason why this great being requires none, may be *his being infinite;* just as space must necessarily have existed, and have been infinite, and without any cause whatever. A difficulty in conceiving *how* a thing can be, is no proof of its impossibility; and indeed there cannot be a clearer instance of it than the present. For nothing can be more evident than that such beings as plants and animals must have had a superior cause; nothing also can be more evident than that they could not have proceeded from each other by succession from all eternity; and therefore nothing can be more evident, than that the primary cause of all these things must himself have existed from all eternity, without any thing prior or superior to him, notwithstanding our utter inability to conceive *how* all this should be.

Since it is evident, from the innumerable marks of design through the whole system of nature, that the author of it is intelligent, and, consequently, had some *end* in view in what he did, let us, in the next place, inquire what this end probably was; and I flatter myself that, instead of meeting with more difficulties in this part of our inquiry, as has often been represented, we shall, in reality, meet with fewer than we have had before; and here analogy, founded on established associations of ideas, is our only guide.

Means and *ends* are perpetually occurring to our observation. Hence no habit is more fixed than that of distinguishing them, and of perceiving the relation they bear to each other. We hardly ever see the hand of man without perceiving marks of design, and they are not less evident in the works of God. That the *eye* was made for seeing, that is, perceiving the form and colour of remote objects, and the *ear* for hearing or perceiving the sounds made by them, is no less evident than that the *pen* and the *ink* with which I write, were made and provided for the purpose of writing.

We are likewise just as able, in many cases, to distinguish a *perfection* from a *defect* in the works of *nature*, as in those of *art*. For the analogy is so great, that we cannot help applying these terms to them, and reasoning in the same manner concerning them. If I go into a mill, and see every wheel in motion, and going with as little friction and noise as possible, I conclude that every thing is as the maker intended it, and that the machine is complete in its kind, answering the end for which it was made. But if I see a pinion break, and the motion of the machine in part obstructed by it, I immediately conclude that this was not intended by the maker, since it must contribute to unfit the machine for its proper functions.

In like manner, judging of the works of God as I do concerning those of man, when I see a plant in its vigour, and an animal of its proper size and form, healthy and strong, I conclude that these are as they were intended to be, and that they are fitted to answer the end of their creation, whatever that was. These, therefore, I attend to, and not to trees that are blighted, or animals that are maimed and diseased, when I wish to form a right judgment of the design of their maker. And, indeed, we do see that, in general, plants and animals are, to a considerable degree, healthy, and that the sickly and diseased among them are exceptions to the general observation.

Now, what is health but a state of *enjoyment* in beings capable of it, and what is *disease* but a diminution of enjoyment, if not a state of actual *pain?* Since then the obvious design of the animal economy was *health*, and not *sickness*, is it not evident that the intention of their maker must have been their *happiness*, not their *misery?* I do not know any conclusion more obvious or more satisfactory than this. What the supreme Author of all things may *farther intend* by the happiness of his creatures, whether a gratification to *himself*, or whether it proceeds from a disinterested regard to *them*, I cannot pretend to judge; but that the happiness of the creation was intended by the author of it, is just as evident as that the design of the millwright was that the wheels of his machine should keep in motion, and not that they should be obstructed.

If, notwithstanding this obvious design, deduced from the consideration of the animal economy, any of them, or all of them, should not be found in a state of actual health and enjoyment, I should rather infer that their author had missed his aim, and was disappointed in what he had in view, than imagine he had not *intended* their health and their happiness: as though I should find that all the mills in my neighbourhood stood still and could not be kept in motion, I should still be satisfied, from their construction, that they were intended to keep in motion, but that the artificer had been disappointed in his object. However, in nature, it is a fact that a state of health, (that is, tolerable though not perfect health,) is general, and a state of sickness comparatively rare. Upon the whole, therefore, the creation is happy though not perfectly so, and the obvious end of the creation is, in fact, in a great measure answered.

It is another argument for the benevolence of the Deity, that many, and perhaps all pains and evils, (the causes of pain,) tend to check and exterminate themselves; whereas, pleasures extend and propagate themselves, and that without limits.

Pain itself is an affection of sentient beings. Now, all sentient beings that we are acquainted with, (in whatever manner that effect is produced,) endeavour to shun pains and procure pleasures, and all the known causes of them. And as our knowledge and power, in this respect, advance with our experience, nothing is wanting to enable us to exterminate all pain and to attain to complete happiness, but a continuance of being.

Mental pains do as certainly tend to check and exterminate themselves as the corporeal ones. For the sensations of shame and remorse always lead us to avoid whatever it be in our conduct that has exposed us to them; and the satisfaction we feel from having acquitted ourselves with integrity and honour, does likewise encourage us to act the part that will best secure the continuance of that most valuable species of human felicity.

Where volition is not concerned, (though the laws of volition are as much as any thing else in the system of nature, the laws of God,) and mere mechanism takes place, it is acknowledged by physicians, that all diseases are the effort of nature to remove some obstruction, something that impedes the animal functions, and thereby to defer the hour of dissolution, and to recover a state of more perfect health and enjoyment; so that nothing is wanting to the removal of all this class of evils but a perfect *conformation*, and sufficient *strength* of those parts of the animal frame in which the disorder is seated, with sufficient *time* for them to discharge their proper functions. But the intention of nature, that is, of the God of nature, who works by general laws, (in which, of course, there are many exceptions,) is the same, whether the animal survive the struggle, which is generally the case, or whether it sink under it. A hundred diseases terminate favourably for one that is fatal. Every cold is the beginning of a fever, but very seldom proceeds so far as to receive so alarming an appellation.

If we look into the external world, we shall see equal reason to be thankful for cold weather, storms and tempests, with every thing else that we sometimes complain of, as far as we are able to understand their real tendency and ultimate effects. And they are not only less evils in lieu of greater, but also, (like the disorders to which the animal frame is subject,) tend to remove some obstruction, and to diffuse more equally, either the *electric matter* or something else, the equal distribution of which is requisite to the good condition of the world.

If we consider *man* the most important object in this part of the creation, we must consider corporeal pleasures as being of the least consequence to his happiness, because intellectual gratifications are evidently of unspeakably more value to him. Man enjoys the time past and future, as well as the present; and, in general, mankind are tolerably happy in this respect, deriving more pleasure than pain from *reflection*. Man always hopes for the best, and even past labour and pain is generally pleasing in recollection, so that whether he looks backwards or forwards, his views are, upon the whole, pleasing.

If we consider man in a moral respect, we shall find that for one man who really suffers from remorse of conscience, numbers think so well of themselves and of their conduct, that it gives them pleasure to reflect upon it; and, in fact, acts of kindness and benevolence far exceed those of cruelty; and in all respects, *moderation*, (which is the standard of virtue,) is much more common than *excess*; and, indeed, if it was not so, excess would not be so much noticed and censured as it is. Upon the whole, virtue seems to bear the same proportion to vice, that happiness does to misery, or health to sickness, in the world.

Besides, to judge of the intention of the Creator, we should not only consider the actual state of things, but take in as much as we can of the *tendencies* of things in future. Now, it requires but little judgment to see that the world is in a state of *melioration* in a variety of respects; and, for the same reason, it will probably continue to improve, and, perhaps, without limits, so that our posterity have a much better prospect before them than we have had.

A great proportion of the misery of man is owing to *ignorance*, and it cannot be denied that the world grows wiser every day. Physicians and surgeons know how much less men suffer now than they did in similar cases formerly, owing to improvements in the science of medicine and in surgical operations. To read of the methods of the ancients, with respect to the stone in the bladder, is enough to fill one with horror. It was not till the time of Celsus, that the practice of extracting the stone was known; and, till of late years, in comparison, it was not expected that one in twenty of those who submitted to the operation would recover; whereas, it is now a tolerably safe operation, and besides, we are not without the hope of discovering methods of dissolving the stone without pain in the bladder. This is only one of many instances of improvements that lessen the sufferings of mankind. This skill is, indeed, in a manner confined to Europeans, but these occupy a considerable part of the globe, and the knowledge of Europeans will, no doubt, gradually extend over the whole world.

Civilization and good government have made great advances in Europe, and by means of this, men live in a state of much greater security and happiness; and even the intercourse between distant places and distant countries is both safe and pleasurable; whereas, in former times, this intercourse was hardly practicable. Let any person read of the state of Italy, and that of the continent of Europe in general in the times of Petrarch, and he will be satisfied that the present state of things is a paradise in comparison with it.

War is unspeakably less dreadful than formerly, though it is a great evil still; and as true political knowledge advances, and the advantages of *commerce*, which supposes a peaceable intercourse, are more experienced, it is fairly to be presumed that wars will not fail to be less frequent, as well as less sanguinary; so that societies of men, as well as families and individuals, will find it to be their common interest to be good neighbours, and national jealousy will give place to national generosity.

The progress of knowledge and other causes, have greatly improved the spirit of the various *religions* that have prevailed in the world. Those peculiarly horrid modes of religion which enjoined human sacrifices, as well as many abominable practices, have been long extinct; and persecution to death for conscience' sake, by which the world suffered so much under the Pagan Roman emperors, and even the philosophical and mild Marcus Aurelius, as well as in the days of Papal tyranny, and under other ecclesiastical hierarchies, we have reason to think will hardly ever be revived, the folly as well as the cruelty of these practices is so generally acknowledged. In consequence of this greater liberty of speculating upon all subjects, truth has a much fairer chance of prevailing in the world, and the knowledge and general spread of truth cannot fail to be attended with a great variety of advantages favourable to the virtue and happiness of mankind.

We have no occasion to consider by what particular *means* these advantages have accrued to mankind; for, whatever the *secondary causes* may have been, they could not have operated without the kind provision of the first and proper cause of all, and therefore they are to be considered as arguments of his benevolence, or of the preference that he gives to happiness before misery.

Upon the whole, the evidence for the *general benevolence* of the Deity seems to be abundantly satisfactory, and all that can be objected on this subject is to the *infinite extent* of it. And yet it should seem that there can be no bounds to an affection that has been proved to be *real*. Why the Divine Being should love his creatures *to a certain degree* and no more, why he should intend them a certain portion of happiness and not a greater, is a question that cannot easily be answered. The probability that an affection unquestionably real is actually unbounded, disposes us to inquire whether, notwithstanding appearances, this may not be the case here. And, though we cannot prove the strict infinity of the divine benevolence, or give so much evidence for it as we can for that of his power and knowledge, yet the probability will, I think, appear to be in favour of it, if we sufficiently attend to the considerations that I shall urge in my next.

I am, &c.

LETTER VI.
Arguments for the Infinite Benevolence of the Deity.

Dear Sir,

Having shewn in my last letter, that the Supreme Cause of all things must be possessed of at least *general benevolence*, in this I shall endeavour to shew that, notwithstanding some seemingly contrary appearances, this benevolence *may*, in a sufficiently proper sense, be considered as *infinite*. For this purpose I would wish you to attend to the following considerations.

First. That any *dependent being* should be at all times infinitely happy must necessarily be impossible, for such a being must be infinitely knowing and powerful, that is, in fact, equal to the Divine Being himself. The happiness of every individual must, therefore, necessarily be *limited*, either in *degree* or by a *mixture of unhappiness;* and whether this necessary limitation is best made in one way or the other, can only be determined by the Deity himself. However, the method of limitation by *a mixture of pain*, will not, I dare say, appear uneligible to persons of competent judgment.

It is even a common thing in human life, to prefer this *variety* rather than an unvaried degree of *moderate enjoyment.* This mode of limitation being supposed preferable, nothing remains to be censured but the *degree* of misery proper or necessary to be mixed with any proportion of happiness, and the *time*, and other *circumstances* of the introduction of this misery. And in this, no person, surely, will pretend to dictate to a Being of infinite wisdom, whose general benevolence is unquestionable. No objection of this kind, therefore, can deserve any reply.

In these respects, however, the probability *a priori*, in general at least, is in favour of what we see actually to take place; so that it is a fair presumption, that, as our experience advances, we shall see more and more reason to be satisfied with the dispensations of Providence: because, in general, we perceive a *gradation* in every thing from worse to better, which is a circumstance highly favourable to happiness, as it encourages *hope,* which is itself a principal ingredient in human happiness. Several improvements in the state of the world in general have been mentioned already, and the like is no less manifest in the case of individuals; the sufferings of our infant state exceeding those that we meet with afterwards, all things considered. Supposing a state of health, and competent subsistence for all, which (being the evident intention of nature) must here be supposed, our enjoyments are continually increasing in real value from infancy to old age. Let a child have the most perfect health, it is impossible to educate him in a proper manner, so as to lay a foundation for his own future happiness, without subjecting him to many disappointments and mortifications, with respect to which, no satisfactory account can be given *him,* so as to make him acquiesce under them. Whereas, besides that the pursuits and enjoyments of manhood are in themselves greatly superior to those of childhood, we acquire by experience such a *comprehension of mind* as enables us to bear without murmuring the evils that fall to our lot; and as this comprehension of mind extends itself every day, supposing what here must also be supposed, (as being within the intention of nature,) a rational and virtuous life, our stock of intellectual enjoyments is augmenting continually, so that the most desirable part of a well-spent life is *old age.* And it is evidently and highly so, provided that, together with health, a man enjoys what is also the intention of nature, the society of a rising and promising family.

The peculiar satisfaction with which a Christian shuts his eyes on the world, will not, perhaps, be thought a proper article in this account; though, whether these hopes be well or ill-founded, they are *actually enjoyed* by great numbers of the human race, and, together with every thing else that actually takes place, must have been intended for us in this life. However, I am well satisfied that a properly natural death, or death occasioned by the mere exhausting (as we may term it) of the vital powers in a sufficient length of time provided no superstitious fears accompany it, is not attended with aversion or pain.

Perhaps no part of the general system will appear at first sight more liable to objection than this circumstance of *death,* and the train of diseases that lead to it. But, by this means, room is made for a *succession of creatures* of each species, so that the *sum of happiness* is, upon the whole, greater. With respect to man, unless the whole plan of his constitution, and all the laws of his nature were changed, it is unspeakably more desirable that there should be a succession, than that the same individuals should continue on the stage always. For a new generation learns wisdom from the follies of the old, which would only have grown more inveterate every year. Thus the whole species advances more quickly to maturity; and to the *species*, the obstinacy, and other infirmities of old age, will probably be ever unknown.

Secondly. Pain itself, and *as such*, is not without its real use, with respect to true happiness, so that, other circumstances (of which we can be no judges) being supposed right, we have reason to be thankful for the pains and distresses to which we are subject. For pain must not be considered only with respect to the moment of sensation, but also as to its future necessary effects; and according to the general law of our nature, admirably explained by Dr. Hartley, the impressions of pain remaining in the mind, fall at length within the limits of pleasure, and contribute most of all to the future enjoyment of life: so that, without this resource, life would necessarily grow insipid and tiresome.

However, without recurring to abstruse considerations, it is well known that the recollection of past troubles, after a certain interval, becomes highly pleasurable; and it is a pleasure of a very durable kind. It is so generally known to be so as to furnish an argument for bearing troubles, and making them less felt at the time of their greatest pressure. Thus Æneas, in Virgil, is represented as saying to his companions in distress, *post hæc meminisse juvabit.**

Nothing can be more evident than the use of pain to children. How is it possible to teach them sufficient caution against absolute destruction, by falls, burns, &c. but by the actual feeling of pain from these circumstances? No parent, or any person who has given much attention to children, will say that admonition alone would answer the purpose; whereas, greater evils are most effectually prevented in the admirable plan of nature, by the actual experience of less evils. What is more pungent than the stings of shame and remorse, in consequence of improprieties in conduct, and of vices? But

---

* Quoted, probably, from memory, instead of *forsan et hæc olim meminisse juvabit.* Æn. i. 203.

could prudence and virtue be effectually inculcated by any other means? No person conversant in the business of education will venture to say that they could.

As the pains and mortifications of our infant state are the natural means of lessening the pains and mortifications of advanced life, so I made it appear to the satisfaction of Dr. Hartley, in the short correspondence I had with him, that his theory furnishes pretty fair presumptions that the pains of this life may suffice for the whole of our future existence, we having now resources enow for a perpetual increase in happiness, without any assistance from the sensation of future pain. This speculation will probably appear before the public in due time, together with other observations relating to the extension and application of this wonderfully simple theory of the mental affections.*

These considerations appear to me abundantly sufficient to convince us that even the unlimited benevolence of the Author of nature is not affected by the partial evils to which we are subject. But still it will be said, that a Being of pure and perfect benevolence might have obviated this inconvenience, by a different original constitution of nature, in which evils might not have been necessary, not being of any use to us, as such.

But, I answer, this is more than we can pretend to say is even *possible*, or within the limits of infinite power itself; and there is this pretty good reason for presuming that it is so, which is, that in present circumstances, we always see, (wherever we can see enough to be in any measure judges,) that the methods that are taken are the best for us, all other things connected with them being considered, and the same *disposition* in our author to provide the best for us in one case would lead him to provide the best for us in another; so that, if *cæteris manentibus*, every thing is for the best, we may conclude that the *whole* is for the best; the disposition of mind to make this provision being the very same in both cases.

Supposing it possible, therefore, for the Divine Being to have created men with all the feelings and ideas that are acquired in the course of a painful and laborious life, since it must have been in violation of all *general laws*, we have reason to conclude that laws, or general methods of acting, are preferable to no laws at all; and

---

* See how this design was frustrated. Vol. III. p. 7, Note.

that it is better, upon the whole, that the divine agency should not be so very conspicuous, as it must have been, upon the plan of a constant and momentary interference.

It is plain there could be little room for the exercise of *wisdom* in God or man, if there had been no general laws. For the whole plan of nature, from which we infer design or wisdom, is admirable, chiefly on account of its being a system of wonderfully general and simple laws, so that innumerable ends are gained by the fewest means, and the greatest good produced with the least possible evil. And the wisdom and foresight of man could have had no scope if there had been no invariable plan of nature to be the object of his investigation and study, by which to guide his conduct and direct his expectations.

In comparison with the solid advantages we derive from the exercise of our faculties on this plan of general laws, how trifling are those that would accrue to us from even the frequent interruption, and much more, from the total abrogation of them. What could we gain but that a child falling into the fire should not be burned, or that a man falling from a precipice should not be dashed to pieces? But all the accidents that happen of this kind, and which our reason is given us to enable us to guard against, are surely not to be bought off at such a price as this. How little do we suffer on the whole by accidents from *fire*, compared with the benefits we derive from it; and how much greater gainers are we still on the balance, by the great *law of gravitation!*

The advantage, if not the necessity of general laws, is best seen in the conduct of a large family, of a school, or of a community, because the good of the whole must be consulted in conjunction with that of each individual; and we often find it to be wise and right to suffer individuals to bring themselves into difficulties, from which we would gladly relieve them, if we had not respect to others who are equally under our care. How often is a favourite child or pupil punished, or an useful member of society falsely convicted of a crime, suffered to die, rather than violate general rules salutary to the whole! Now, as small societies cannot be governed without general rules and particular inconveniences, it may, for any thing that we know, be naturally impossible to govern the large society of mankind without such general laws, though attended with particular inconveniencies.

If it be said that the Divine Being might *conceal* his violation of the laws of nature for the benefit of individuals, I answer that those individuals would, without a second interference, lose the benefit they would have derived from their sufferings, as such (teaching them caution, &c.); and if the Divine Being did this in all cases to prevent all evil, there would be no general laws at all; and who can direct him when to interfere and when not? As to very rare cases, it is possible, though I own not probable, because it would imply a want of foresight in the original plan, that the Divine Being does interfere in this invisible manner.

If we consider the human race as the most valuable of the divine productions on the face of the earth, and intellectual happiness as the most valuable part of their happiness; if the training of men to get elevation of thought, comprehension of mind, virtuous affections and generous actions, be any object with the great Author of all things, (and the good of the whole seems to require that there should be a proportion of such exalted beings,) this world, with all its imperfections, as we think them, is perhaps the best possible school in which they could be thus trained. How could we be taught compassion for others, without suffering ourselves, and where could the rudiments of the heroic virtues of fortitude, patience, clemency, &c. be acquired but in the school of adversity, in struggling with hardships, and contending with oppression, ingratitude, and other vices, moral evils as well as natural ones?

If we suppose these truly great minds formed here as in a *nursery*, for the purposes of future existence respecting their own happiness or that of others, the consideration will furnish another argument for the present state of things. What evidence there is of this being the case we shall see hereafter.

Upon the whole, it is very possible, notwithstanding some appearances to the contrary, that the affection of the Universal Parent to his offspring may be even *boundless*, or, properly speaking, *infinite*, and also that the actual happiness of the whole creation may be considered as infinite, notwithstanding all the partial evil there is in it. For if good prevail upon the whole, the creation being supposed infinite, happiness will be infinitely extended; and in the eye of a being of perfect comprehension, such as the Divine Being must be, capable of perceiving the balance of good only, it will be happiness unmixed with misery. Nay, supposing men, (and it is of men only that I am now treating,) to live for ever, if each be happy upon the whole, and especially if the happiness of each be constantly accelerated, each individual may be said to be infinitely happy in the whole of his existence, so that to the divine comprehension, the whole will be happiness *infinito-infinite*. See Dr. Hartley's admirable illustration of this subject, in the second volume of his *Observations on Man*, Prop. iv.

I am, &c.

LETTER VII.

The Evidence of the Moral Government of the World, and the Branches of Natural Religion.

Dear Sir,

If you will admit that I have proved to your satisfaction that there is a God, a first cause, possessed of infinite power, wisdom and goodness, or only of such degrees of those attributes as, in a popular sense of the word, may be deemed infinite, that is, far exceeding our comprehension, nothing more will be requisite to prove every moral perfection, and that we are under a proper *moral government*.

Justice, mercy and veracity, with every thing else that is of a *moral nature*, are in fact, and philosophically considered, only modifications of benevolence. For a Being, simply and truly *benevolent*, will necessarily act according to what are called the rules of *justice*, *mercy* and *veracity*, because in no other way can he promote the good of such moral agents as are subject to his government. Even *justice* itself, which seems to be the most opposite to goodness, is such a degree of severity, or pains and penalties so inflicted, as will produce the best effect, with respect both to those who are exposed to them, and to others who are under the same government; or, in other words, that degree of evil which is calculated to produce the greatest degree of good: and if the punishment exceed this measure, if, in any instance, it be an *unnecessary* or *useless suffering*, it is always censured as *cruelty*, and it is not even called justice, but real injustice.

For the same reason, if, in any particular case, the strict execution of the law would do more harm than good, it is universally agreed that the punishment ought to be remitted, and then what we call *mercy* or clemency will take place; but it does not deserve the name of clemency, nor is it worthy of commendation as a virtue, but it is censured as a weakness, or something worse, if it be so circumstanced as to encourage the commission of crimes, and, consequently, make more suffering necessary in future. In short, a truly good and wise governor frames the whole of his administration with a view to the happiness of his subjects, or he will endeavour to produce the greatest sum of happiness with the least possible mixture of pain or misery.

But you will check me in the course of this argument, and say that if moral government be the necessary result of benevolence, we ought to perceive some traces of this moral government before we can admit the Supreme Being to be benevolent, and that this ought to be the principal argument for his benevolence.

I acknowledge it, but at the same time I must observe that any independent evidence of benevolence, such as I have produced, is a strong proof, *a priori*, that there will be a moral government; because, as I have just shewn, if benevolence be uniform and consistent, it must produce moral government where moral agents are concerned, so that, having this previous reason to expect a moral government, we ought to suppose that such a government *does* exist, unless there be evident proof of the contrary: because if this proof be indisputable, it must be concluded that the Supreme Being is benevolent, of which we are supposed to have already other independent evidence.

Now, the mere *delay of punishment*, which is all that we can allege against the reality of a present moral government, is no evidence against it, so long as the offender is within the reach of justice, because it may be an instance of the wisdom and just discretion of a governor to give all his subjects a sufficient *trial*, and treat them according to their *general character*, allowing sufficient time in which to form that character, rather than exact an immediate punishment for every particular offence.

It is no uncommon thing with *men* not to punish for the first offence, but to give room for amendment; and it may be the more expected of *God*, whose justice no criminal can finally escape, and whose penetration no artifice can impose upon. Had human magistrates more knowledge and more power, they might, in that proportion, give greater scope to men to form and to shew their characters, by deferring to take cognizance of crimes. It is because criminals may impose upon them by pretences of reformation, or escape from their hands, that it is, in general, wise in them to animadvert upon crimes without much delay, and with few exceptions.

For any thing that appears, therefore, the present state of the world, notwithstanding, in some respects, *all things fall alike to all,* and a visible distinction is not always made between the righteous and the wicked; and even, notwithstanding the wicked may, in some cases, derive an advantage from their vices, may perfectly correspond to such a state of moral government as a Being of infinite wisdom and power would exercise towards mankind. And if this only *may* be the case, any independent evidence of the divine benevolence ought to make us conclude that this *is* the case, and lead us to expect that, at a proper time, (of which the Divine Being himself is the only judge,) both the righteous and the wicked will meet with their just and full recompense.

But there is not wanting *independent* and sufficient evidence of a moral government of the world, similar to the independent evidence of the benevolence of its author. For, notwithstanding what has been admitted above, respecting the promiscuous distribution of happiness and misery in the world, it is unquestionable, that virtue gives a man a better chance for happiness than vice.

What happiness can any man enjoy without *health?* And is not temperance favourable to health, and intemperance the bane of it? What are all the outward advantages of life without *peace of mind?* And, whatever be the proximate cause of it, it is a fact, and therefore must have been the intention of our Maker, that peace of mind is the natural companion of integrity and honour, and not of fraud and injustice. It is the fruit of benevolence, and of that course of conduct which arises from it, and by no means of malevolence. Do we not also see that a moderate competency, which is much more valuable than riches, is generally the reward of fidelity and industry, and that possessions acquired by dishonest arts are very insecure, if, on other accounts, a man could have any enjoyment of them. What but common observation has given rise to the common proverb, that *honesty is the best policy?*

The best definition and criterion of virtue, is that disposition of mind, and that course of conduct arising from it, which is best calculated to promote a man's own happiness and the happiness of others with whom he is connected; and to prove any thing to be really and ultimately mischievous, is the same thing as to prove it to be vicious and wrong. The rule of temperance is to eat and drink so as to lay a foundation for health, and consequently enjoyment; and intemperance does not consist in the pleasure we receive from the gratification of our appetites, but in procuring momentary pleasure with future and more lasting pain, in laying a foundation for diseases, and thereby disqualifying a man for enjoying life himself, or contributing to the happiness of others who are dependent upon him. In the same manner we fix the boundaries of all the vices and all the virtues. Virtue is, in fact, that which naturally produces the greatest sum of good, and vice is that which produces the greatest sum of evil.

In short, the virtuous man is he that acts with the greatest wisdom and comprehension of mind, having respect to what is future as well as what is present; and the vicious man is he that acts with the least just prudence and foresight, catching at present pleasure and advantage, and neglecting what is future, though of more value to him. It cannot, therefore, but be, that virtue must, upon the whole, lead to happiness and vice to misery; and since this arises from the constitution of nature and of the world, it must have been the intention of the Author of nature that it should be so.

Also, as from the *general* benevolence of the Deity we inferred his *infinite* benevolence, so from his general respect to virtue we may infer his strict and invariable respect to it; and as it cannot but appear probable that partial evils must be admitted by an all-powerful, and certainly a benevolent Being, because they may be, in a manner unknown to us, connected with, or productive of good, so there is an equal probability that, in the administration of a Being of infinite power and wisdom, and certainly a favourer of virtue as of happiness, all irregularities in the distribution of rewards and punishments are either only seemingly so or merely temporary; and that, when the whole scheme shall be completed, they will appear to have been proper parts of the most perfect moral administration.

Since then, it is a fact that we are in a state justly entitled to the appellation of *moral government,* (this being not only presumed from the consideration of the divine benevolence previously established, but also deduced independently from actual appearances,) there must be a foundation for what may be termed *natural religion,* that is, there is a system of *duty* to which we ought to conform, because there are *rewards and punishments* that we have to expect.

Our duty with respect to *ourselves* and *others* is, in general, sufficiently obvious, because it is, in fact, nothing more than to *feel* and to *act* as our own true and ultimate happiness, in conjunction with that of others, requires. With respect to the *Divine Being*, we must be guided by analogies, which, however, are tolerably distinct.

Thus, if gratitude be due to human benefactors, it must be due in a greater degree to God, from whom we receive unspeakably more than from man; and, in like manner, it must be concluded to be our duty to reverence him, to respect his authority, and to confide in the wisdom and goodness of his providence. For since he made us, it must be evident that we are not beneath his notice and attention; and since all the laws of nature to which we are subject, are his establishment, nothing that befals us can be unforeseen, or, consequently, unintended by him. With this persuasion, we must see and respect the hand of God in every thing. And if every thing is as God intended it to be, it is the same thing to us whether this intention was formed the moment immediately preceding any particular event, or from all eternity.

If reverence, gratitude, obedience and confidence be our duty with respect to God, (which we infer from the analogy of those duties to men,) it is agreeable to the same analogy that we *express* these sentiments in words; and this is done in the most natural manner agreeably to the same analogy, in a direct *address* to the Author of our being, so that the principles of natural religion, properly pursued, will lead us to *prayer*.

That we should express our reverence for God, our gratitude to him, and our confidence in him, is generally thought reasonable; but it is said that we are not authorized to *ask* any thing of him. But even this is unavoidable, if we follow the analogy above-mentioned. Considering God as our governor, father, guardian or protector, we cannot resist the impulse to apply to him in our difficulties, as to any other being or person standing in the same relation to us. Analogy sets aside all distinction in this case, and if the analogy itself be natural, it is itself a part of the constitution of nature, and, therefore, sufficiently authorizes whatever is agreeable to it.

It is no objection to the natural duty of prayer to God that he is supposed to know our wants, and to be the best judge of the propriety of supplying them. For we ourselves may have the same good disposition towards our children, and yet see sufficient reason for insisting upon their personal application to us, as an expression of their obligation, and a necessary means of cultivating a due sense of their relation to us, and dependence upon us.

The idea of every thing being *predetermined* from all eternity, is no objection to prayer, because all *means* are appointed as well as *ends;* and, therefore, if prayer be in itself a proper means, the end to be obtained by it, we may be assured, will not be had without *this* any more than without any other means, or other necessary previous circumstances. No man will refrain from plowing his ground because God foresees whether he will have a harvest or not. It is sufficient for us to know that there never has been, and therefore, probably never will be any harvest without previous plowing. Knowing this, if we only have the desire of harvest, plowing the ground, and every thing else that we know to be previously necessary to it, and to be *within our power*, will be done by us of course.

It is possible, however, that were we as perfect as our nature and state will admit, having acquired all the comprehension of mind to which we can ever attain, and having a steady belief in the infinite wisdom, power and goodness of God, with a constant sense of his presence with us, and unremitted attention to us, our devotion might be nothing more than a deep *reverence* and joyful *confidence*, persuaded that all the divine disposals were right and kind ; and in their calmer moments very excellent and good men *do* approach to this state. They feel no occasion to *ask* for any thing, because they feel *no want* of any thing. But the generality of mankind always, and the best of men not possessing themselves at all times with equal tranquillity, must and will acquiesce in a devotion of a less perfect form. And the Divine Being, knowing this imperfect state of our nature, must *mean* that we should act agreeably to it, and *require* of us expressions of devotion adapted to our imperfect state.

This progress is also agreeable to the analogy of nature: for when our children are fully possessed of that affection for us, and confidence in us, which was the object and end of any formal prescribed mode of address, &c. we do not insist upon the *form*. We are then satisfied with their experienced attachment to us, and make them equally the objects of our kind attention, whether they apply to us in form for what they want or not.

In all this, you see, we must content ourselves with

following the best analogies we can find, and those are clearly in favour of a *duty to God* as well as to man; and for the same reason, a duty and a behaviour similar to that which we acknowledge to be due to our parents, guardians and friends, but differing in proportion to the infinite superiority of the Supreme Being to every inferior being, and the infinitely greater magnitude of our obligations to him. Let us now see whether there be any analogy, from the common course of nature, that can give us any insight into the *extent* and *duration* of the system of moral government under which we manifestly are. But this I shall reserve for the subject of another letter. In the mean time,

I am, &c.

LETTER VIII.
Of the Evidence for the future Existence of Man.

DEAR SIR,

I HAVE already observed that benevolence, once proved to be *real*, can hardly be conceived to be other than *boundless;* and this must be more especially the case with the Supreme Being, who can have no rival, or be jealous of any being whatever. Such beings as *we* are may really wish well to others, and yet may wish them only a *certain degree* of happiness; but then the desire of that limitation will be found, if it be examined, to be occassioned by something peculiar to our situation, as limited and imperfect beings, and what can have no place with the Deity. His benevolence, if real, must, as we should think, be boundless. He must, therefore, wish the greatest good of his creation, and the limitation to the present *actual happiness* of the universe must arise from *perfection of happiness* being incompatible with the nature of created, and, consequently, finite beings, and with that mixture of pain, which may be really necessary, according to the best possible general constitution of nature, to promote this happiness.

But pain, we have seen, tends to limit and exclude itself, and things are evidently in a progress to a better state. There is some reason, therefore, to expect that this *melioration* will go on without limits. And as exact and equal government arises from perfect benevolence, (and even, independent of the arguments for benevolence, does take place in some degree,) we cannot, as it should seem, but be led by this analogy to expect a more perfect retribution than we see to take place here, and, consequently, to look for a state where moral agents will find more exact rewards for virtue, and more ample punishments for vice, than they meet with in this world. I do not say that the argument from these analogies is so strong as to produce a *confident expectation* of such a future state ; but it certainly, in fact, produces a *wish* for it ; and this wish itself, being produced by the analogy of nature, is some evidence of the thing wished for.

Other analogies, it is acknowledged, tend to damp this expectation. We see that men, whose powers of perception and thought depend upon the organized state of the brain, decay and die, exactly like plants, or the inferior animals, and we see no instance of any revival. But still, while there exists in nature a power unquestionably equal to their revival, (for it is the power that actually brought them into being at first,) the former analogies may lead us to look for this future state of more exact retribution, to which we see something like a reference, in this, and for a more copious display of the divine goodness, even beyond the grave.

On some, especially on persons conscious of great integrity, and of great sufferings in consequence of it, these analogies will make a greater impression, will produce a more earnest *longing*, and, consequently, a stronger *faith*, than others will have ; and the same persons will, for the same reason, be affected by them differently at different times. This fluctuation, and degree of uncertainty, must make every rational being, and especially every good man, who rejoices in what he sees of the works and government of God, earnestly long for farther information on this most interesting subject ; and this farther information we may perhaps find the Universal Father has actually given us.

I think it of some importance to observe, that the degree of moral government under which we are (the constitution of nature evidently favouring a course of virtue, and frowning upon a course of vice) is a *fact* independent of all reasoning concerning the existence of God himself, and, therefore, ought to determine the conduct of those who are not satisfied with respect to the proof of the being and attributes of God, and even of those who are properly *atheists*, believing that nothing exists besides the world, or the universe, of which we ourselves are a part.

Whether there be any *author of nature*, or not, there cannot be any doubt of there being *an established course of nature;* and an atheist must believe it to be the more firmly established, and see less prospect of any change, from acknowledging no superior being capable of producing that change. If, therefore, the course of nature be actually in favour of virtue, it must be the interest and wisdom of every human being to be virtuous. And farther, if it be agreeable to the analogy of nature, independent of any consideration of the author of it, that things are in an improving state, and, consequently, that there is a tendency to a more exact and equal retribution, it must produce an expectation that this course of nature will *go on* to favour virtue still more; and, therefore, it may be within the course of nature that men, as *moral agents*, should survive the grave, or be *re-produced*, to enjoy the full reward of virtue, or to suffer the punishments due to their vices.

It is acknowledged that we have no idea *how* this can come to pass, but neither have we any knowledge how we, that is, the human species, came into being; so that, for any thing we know to the contrary, our *re-production* may be as much within the proper course of nature, as our original production; and consequently, nothing hinders but that our expectation of a more perfect state of things, and a state of more exact retribution, raised by the observation of the actual course of nature, may be fulfilled. There may, therefore, be *a future state*, even though there be no God at all. That is, as it is certainly, and independently of all other considerations, our wisdom to be virtuous in this life, it may be equally our wisdom to be virtuous with a view to a life to come. And, faint as this probability may be thought, it is however *something*, and must add something to the sanctions of virtue. Let not atheists, therefore, think themselves *quite secure* with respect to a future life. Things as extraordinary as this, especially upon the hypothesis of there being no God, have taken place, and therefore this, which is sufficiently analogous to the rest, *may* take place also.

Let any person only consider attentively the meanest plant that comes in his way, and he cannot but discover a wonderful *extent of view* in the adaptation of every part of it to the rest, as of the root to the stem, the stem to the leaf, the leaf to the flower, the flower to the fruit, the fruit to the seed, &c. &c. &c. He will also perceive as wonderful an adaptation of all these to the soil and the climate, and to the destined duration, mode and extent of propagation, &c. of the plant. He will also perceive a wonderful relation of one plant to another, with respect to similarity of structure, uses and mutual subserviency. He will perceive another relation that they bear to the animals that feed upon them, or, in any other respect, avail themselves of them. In extending his researches, he will perceive an equal extent of view in the parts of the animal economy, their relation to the vegetable world, and to one another, as of the carnivorous to the graminivorous, &c. and of every thing belonging to them, to their rank, place and use, in the system of the world.

After this, let him consider this world, that is, the earth, as part of a greater system, (each part of which, probably, as perfect in its kind,) with the probable relation of the solar system itself to other systems in the visible universe. And then, whether he supposes that there is any *author of nature*, or not, he must see that, *by some means or other*, nothing is ever wanting, however remote in time or place, to render every thing *complete in its kind.* And if his mind be sufficiently impressed with these *facts*, and the consideration of the many events that daily take place, of which he could not have the least previous expectation, and of the efficient or proximate causes of which he is wholly ignorant, and he will not think it impossible, that, if any other particular event, of whatever magnitude, even the reproduction of the whole human race after a certain period, will make the system *more complete*, even that event may take place, though he be ever so ignorant of the proximate cause of it. That there is both a *power* in nature, and an *extent of view*, abundantly adequate to it, if he have any knowledge of *actual existence*, he must be satisfied. In proportion, therefore, to his idea of the *propriety* and *importance* of any future state of things, in that proportion will be his *expectation* of it. Our ignorance of the *means* by which any particular future state of things may be brought about, is balanced by our acknowledged ignorance of the means in other cases, where the result is indisputable ; though we are continually advancing in the discovery of these means, in our investigation of the more general laws of nature.

A retrospective view to our former ignorance in other cases will be useful to us here. Time was, when the total solution of a piece of metal in a chemical *menstruum* would seem to be as absolute a *loss* of it, as the dissolution of a human body by putrefaction, and the recovery of it would have been thought as hopeless. And, antecedent to our knowledge of the course of nature, the burying of a seed in the earth would seem to have as little tendency to the re-production of the plant. Where there certainly exists a power equal to any production, or any event, any thing that is *possible in itself* may be, and the difference in *antecedent probability* is only that of greater and less.

I am, &c.

LETTER IX.

An Examination of Mr. Hume's DIALOGUES ON NATURAL RELIGION.

Dear Sir,

I am glad to find that you think there is at least some appearance of weight in what, at your request, I have urged, in answer to the objections against the belief of a God and a providence; and I am confident the more attention you give to the subject, the stronger will those arguments appear, and the more trifling and undeserving of regard you will think the cavils of atheists, ancient or modern. You wish, however, to know distinctly what I think of *Mr. Hume's posthumous Dialogues on Natural Religion;* * because, coming from a writer of some note, that work is frequently a topic of conversation in the societies you frequent.

With respect to *Mr. Hume's metaphysical writings* in general, my opinion is, that, on the whole, the world is very little the wiser for them. For though, when the merits of any question were on his side, few men ever wrote with more perspicuity, the arrangement of his thoughts being natural, and his illustrations peculiarly happy; yet I can hardly think that we are indebted to him for the least real advance in the knowledge of the human mind. Indeed, according to his own very frank confession, his object was mere *literary reputation.*† It was not the *pursuit of truth,* or the advancement of virtue and happiness; and it was much more easy to make a figure by disturbing the systems of others, than by erecting any of his own. All schemes have their respective weak sides, which a man who has nothing of his own to risk may more easily find, and expose.

In many of his *Essays* (which, in general, are excessively wire-drawn) Mr. Hume seems to have had nothing in view

---

* "Dialogues concerning Natural Religion. By David Hume, Esq." 1779. Ed. 2.

† See his *Life*, written by himself, 1777, pp. 32, 33. *(P.)*

but to *amuse* his readers, which he generally does agreeably enough; proposing doubts to received hypotheses, leaving them without any solution, and altogether unconcerned about it. In short, he is to be considered in these *Essays* as a mere *writer* or *declaimer*, even more than Cicero in his book of Tusculan Questions.

He seems not to have given himself the trouble so much as to read *Dr. Hartley's Observations on Man*, a work which he could not but have heard of, and which it certainly behoved him to study. The doctrine of *association of ideas*, as explained and extended by Dr. Hartley, supplies materials for the most satisfactory solution of almost all the difficulties he has started, as I could easily shew if I thought it of any consequence; so that to a person acquainted with this theory of the human mind, *Hume's Essays* appear the merest trifling. Compared with Dr. Hartley, I consider Mr. Hume as not even a child.

Now, I will frankly tell you, that this last performance of Mr. Hume has by no means changed for the better the idea I had before formed of him as a metaphysical writer. The dialogue is ingeniously and artfully conducted. *Philo*, who evidently speaks the sentiments of the writer, is not made to say all the good things that are advanced, his opponents are not made to say any thing that is very palpably absurd, and every thing is made to pass with great decency and decorum.

But though *Philo*, in the most interesting part of the debate, advances nothing but common-place objections against the belief of a God, and hackneyed declamation against the plan of providence, his antagonists are seldom represented as making any satisfactory reply. And when, at the last, evidently to save appearances, he relinquishes the argument, on which he had expatiated with so much triumph, it is without alleging any sufficient reason; so that his arguments are left, as no doubt the writer intended, to have their full effect on the mind of the reader. Also, though the debate seemingly closes in favour of the theist, the victory is clearly on the side of the atheist. I therefore shall not be surprised if this work should have a considerable effect in promoting the cause of atheism, with those whose *general turn of thinking* and *habits of life* make them no ill-wishers to that scheme.

To satisfy your wishes, I shall recite what I think has most of the appearance of strength or plausibility, in what Mr. Hume has advanced on the atheistical side of the question, though it will necessarily lead me to repeat some things that I have observed already; but I shall endeavour to do it in such a manner, that you will not deem it quite idle and useless repetition.

With respect to the general argument for the being of God, from the marks of design in the universe, he says, " Will any man tell me, with a serious countenance, that an orderly universe must arise from some thought and art, like the human, because we have experience of it? To ascertain this reasoning, it were requisite that we had experience of the origin of worlds, and it is not sufficient, surely, that we have seen ships and cities arise from human art and contrivance." Pp. 65, 66.

Now, if it be admitted that there are marks of design in the universe, as numberless fitnesses of things to things prove beyond all dispute, is it not a necessary consequence, that if it had a cause at all, it must be one that is capable of design? Will any person say that an eye could have been constructed by a being who had no knowledge of optics, who did not know the nature of light, or the laws of refraction? And must not the universe have had a cause, as well as any thing else, that is finite and incapable of comprehending itself?

We might just as reasonably say, that any particular ship, or city, any particular horse, or man, had nothing existing superior to it, as that the visible universe had nothing superior to it, if the universe be no more capable of comprehending itself than a ship, or a city, a horse, or a man. There can be no charm in the words *world* or *universe*, so that they should require no cause when they stand in precisely the same predicament with other things that evidently *do* require a superior cause, and could not have existed without one.

All that Mr. Hume says on the difficulty of stopping at the idea of an uncaused being, is on the supposition that this uncaused being is a *finite one*, incapable of comprehending itself, and, therefore, in the same predicament with a ship or a house, a horse or a man, which it is impossible to conceive to have existed without a superior cause. " How shall we satisfy ourselves," says he, " concerning the cause of that Being whom you suppose the author of nature? If we stop and go no farther, why go so far? Why not stop at the material world? How can we satisfy ourselves without going on *in infinitum?*—By supposing it to contain the principle of its order within itself, we really assert it to be God, and the sooner we arrive at that Divine Being, so much the better. When you go one step beyond the mundane system, you only excite an inquisitive humour, which it is impossible ever to satisfy." Pp. 93—95.

It is very true, that no person can satisfy himself with going backwards *in infinitum* from one thing that requires a superior cause, to another that equally requires a superior cause. But any person may be sufficiently satisfied with going back through finite causes as far as he has evidence of the existence of intermediate finite causes; and then, seeing that it is absurd to go on *in infinitum* in this manner, to conclude that, whether he can comprehend it or not, there *must* be some *uncaused intelligent Being*, the original and designing cause of all other beings. For, otherwise, what we *see* and *experience* could not have existed. It is true that we cannot conceive *how* this should be, but we are able to acquiesce in this ignorance, because there is no *contradiction* in it.

He says, " Motion, in many instances from gravity, from elasticity, from electricity, begins in matter without any known voluntary agent; and to suppose always in these cases an unknown voluntary agent, is mere hypothesis, and hypothesis attended with no advantages." P. 147. He also says, " Why may not motion have been propagated by impulse through all eternity?" P. 148.

I will admit that the powers of gravity, elasticity and electricity, might have been in bodies from all eternity, without any superior cause, if the bodies in which we find them were capable of knowing that they had such powers, of that *design* which has proportioned them to one another, and of combining them in the wonderful and useful manner in which they are actually proportioned and combined in nature. But when I see that they are as evidently incapable of this as I am of properly producing a plant or an animal, I am under a necessity of looking for a higher cause; and I cannot rest till I come to a being *essentially different* from all visible beings whatever, so as not to be in the predicament that they are in, of requiring a superior cause. Also, if motion could have been in the universe without any cause, it must have been in consequence of bodies being possessed of the power of *gravity*, &c. from eternity, without a cause. But as they could not have had those powers without communication from a superior and intelligent being, capable of proportioning them in the exact and useful manner in which they are possessed, the thing is manifestly *impossible*.

What Mr. Hume says with respect to the *origin of the world* in the following paragraph, which I think unworthy of a philosopher, and miserably trifling on so serious a subject, goes entirely upon the idea of the supreme cause resembling such beings as do themselves require a superior cause, and not (which, however, *must* be the case) a being that can have no superior in wisdom or power. I, therefore, think it requires no particular animadversion.

" Many worlds," he says, " might have been botched and bungled throughout an eternity, ere this system was struck out, much labour lost, many fruitless trials made, and a slow, but continued improvement, carried on during infinite ages in the art of world making." P. 107.

" A man who follows your hypothesis, is able perhaps to assert, or conjecture, that the universe some time arose from something like design; but beyond that position he cannot ascertain one single circumstance, and is left afterwards to fix every point of his theology by the utmost licence of fancy and hypothesis. This world, for ought he knows, is very faulty and imperfect, compared to a superior standard, and was only the first rude essay of some infant deity, who afterwards abandoned it, ashamed of his lame performance. It is the work only of some dependent inferior deity; and is the object of derision to his superiors. It is the production of old age and dotage, in some superannuated deity, and ever since his death has run on at adventures, from the first impulse and active force, which it received from him." Pp. 111, 112.

In reading *Mr. Hume's Life*, written by himself, one might be surprised to find no mention of a *God*, or of a *providence*, which conducted him through it; but this cannot be any longer wonderful, when we find that, for any thing he certainly believed to the contrary, he himself might be the most considerable being in the universe. His maker, if he had any, might have been either a careless playful infant, a trifling forgetful dotard, or was, perhaps, dead and buried, without leaving any other to take care of his affairs. All that he believed of his maker was, that he was capable of *something like design*, but of his own comprehensive intellectual powers he could have no doubt.

Neither can we think it at all extraordinary that Mr. Hume should have recourse to *amusing books* in the last period of his life, when he considered the Author of nature himself as never having had any serious object in view, and when he neither left any thing behind him, nor had any thing before him that was deserving of his care. How can it be supposed that the man, who scrupled not to ridicule his maker, should consider the human race, or the world, in any other light than as objects of ridicule or pity? And well satisfied might he be to have been so fortunate in his passage through the world, and his easy escape out of it, when it was deserted by its maker, and was continually exposed to some unforeseen and dreadful catastrophe. How poor a consolation, however, must have been his *literary fame* with such gloomy prospects as these!

What Mr. Hume says with respect to the deficiency in the proof of the *proper infinity* of the divine attributes, and of a probable *multiplicity of deities*, all goes on the same idea, viz. that the ultimate cause of the universe is such a being as must himself require a superior cause; whereas, nothing can be more evident, how incomprehensible soever it may be, than that the Being which has existed from eternity, and is the cause of all that does exist, must be one that *cannot* have a superior, and, therefore, must be infinite in knowledge and power, and consequently, as I have endeavoured to shew before, can be but *one*.

" As the cause," he says, " ought only to be proportioned to the effect, and the effect, so far as it falls under our cognizance, is not infinite; what pretensions have we —to ascribe that attribute to the Divine Being?—By sharing the work among several we may so much farther limit the attributes of each, and get rid of that extensive power and knowledge which must be supposed in one deity." Pp. 104, 105, 108. This I think unworthy of a philosopher on so grave and interesting a subject.

It is owing to the same inattention to this one consideration, that, in order to get rid of the idea of a supreme intelligent cause of all things, Mr. Hume urges the superior probability of the universe resembling a *plant*, or an *animal*. " If the universe," says he, " bears a greater likeness to animal bodies and to vegetables, than to the works of human art, it is more probable that its cause resembles the cause of the former than that of the latter; and its origin ought rather to be ascribed to generation or vegetation, than to reason or design." P. 129.

On this, *Demea*, the orthodox speaker, very properly observes, " Whence could arise so wonderful a faculty but from design, or how can order spring from any thing which perceives not that order which it bestows?" P. 137. In reply to which, *Philo* contents himself with saying, " A tree bestows order and organization, on that tree which springs from it, without knowing the order; an animal, in the same manner, on its offspring." Ibid. And " Judging by our limited and imperfect experience, generation has some privileges above reason; for we see every day the latter arise from the former, never the former from the latter." P. 140.

Manifestly unsatisfactory as this reply is, nothing is advanced in answer to it by either of the other disputants. But it is obvious to remark, that, if an animal has marks of design in its construction, a design which itself cannot comprehend, it is hardly possible for any person to imagine that it was originally produced without a power superior to itself, and capable of comprehending its structure, though he was not himself present at the original formation of it, and, therefore, could not see it. Can we possibly believe that any particular *horse* that we know, originated without a superior cause? Equally impossible is it to believe, that the *species of horses* should have existed without a superior cause.

How little then does it avail Mr. Hume to say, that " reason, instinct, generation, vegetation,—are similar to each other, and are the causes of similar effects;" p. 135, as if *instinct, generation* and *vegetation*, did not necessarily imply *design* or reason as the cause of them. He might with equal reason have placed other powers in nature, as *gravity, elasticity*, &c. in the same rank with these; whereas, all these must equally have proceeded from reason or design, and could not have had any existence independent of it. For design is conspicuous in all those powers, and especially in the proportion and distribution of them.

Pursuing the analogy of plants and animals, he says, " In like manner as a tree sheds it seeds into the neighbouring fields and produces other trees, so the great vegetable, the world, or this planetary system, produces within itself certain seeds, which, being scattered into the surrounding chaos, vegetate into new worlds. A comet, for instance, is the seed of a world, and after it has been fully ripened by passing from sun to sun, and star to star, it is at last tossed into the unformed elements, which every where surround this universe, and immediately sprouts up into a new system." P. 132.

" Or, if—we should suppose this world to be an *animal;* a comet is the *egg* of this animal; and in like manner as an ostrich lays its egg in the sand, which, without any farther care, hatches the egg, and produces a new animal; so, does not a plant or an animal, which springs from vegetation or generation, bear a stronger resemblance to the world, than does any artificial machine, which arises from reason and design?" Pp. 132—134.

Had any friend of religion advanced an idea so completely absurd as this, what would not Mr. Hume have said to turn it into ridicule! With just as much probability might he have said that Glasgow grew from a seed yielded by Edinburgh, or that London and Edinburgh, marrying, by natural generation, produced York, which lies between them. With much more probability might he have said that *pamphlets* are the productions of large *books,* that *boats* are young *ships,* and that *pistols* will grow into great *guns;* and that either there never were any first towns, books, ships, or guns, or that, if there were, they had no makers.

How it could come into any man's head to imagine that a thing so complex as this world, consisting of land and water, earths and metals, plants and animals, &c. &c. &c. should produce a seed, or egg, containing within it the elements of all its innumerable parts, is beyond my power of conception.

What must have been that man's knowledge of philosophy and nature, who could suppose for a moment, that a comet could possibly be the seed of a world? Do comets spring from worlds, carrying with them the seeds of all the plants, &c. that they contain? Do comets travel from sun to sun, or from star to star? By what force are they tossed into the *unformed elements,* which Mr. Hume supposes every where to surround the universe? What are those elements; and what evidence has he of their existence? Or, supposing the comet to arrive among them, whence could arise its power of vegetating into a new system? What analogy is there in any of those wild suppositions to any thing that actually exists?

What Mr. Hume objects to the arguments for the *benevolence* of the Deity is such mere cavilling, and admits of such easy answers, that I am surprised that a man, whose sole object was even *literary reputation,* should have advanced it.

" The course of nature tends not to human or animal felicity, therefore it is not established for that purpose."

P. 186. He might as well have said that *health* is not agreeable to the course of nature, as that enjoyment and *happiness* is not, since the one is the necessary consequence of the other. It "is contrary," he says, in fact, "to every one's feeling and experience" to "maintain a continued existence in this world—to be eligible and desirable.—It is contrary to an authority so established as nothing can subvert." P. 193. And yet almost all animals and all men *do* desire life, and, according to his own account, his own life was a singularly happy and enviable one.

"You must prove these pure unmixed and uncontroullable attributes from the present mixed and confused phenomena, and from these alone. A hopeful undertaking!" P. 195. If *evil* was not, in a thousand ways, necessarily connected with, and subservient to *good*, the undertaking would be hopeless, but not otherwise.

"It seems plainly possible to carry on the business of life without any pain. Why then is any animal ever rendered susceptible of such a sensation?" P. 205. But pain, *as such*, we have seen to be excellently useful, as a guard against more pain and greater evils, and also as an element of future happiness; and no man can pretend to say that the same end *could* have been attained by any other means.

"The conducting of the world by general laws—seems no wise necessary to a very perfect being." P. 206. But without general laws there could have been little or no room for *wisdom* in God or man; and what kind of happiness could we have had without the exercise of our rational powers? To have had any *intellectual enjoyments* in those circumstances (and the sensual are of little value in comparison with them), we must have been beings of quite another kind than we are at present, probably much inferior to what we are now.

"Almost all the moral as well as natural evils of human life arise from *idleness*; and were our species, by the original constitution of their frame, exempt from this vice, or infirmity, the perfect cultivation of land, the improvement of arts and manufactures, the exact execution of every office and duty, immediately follow; and men at once may fully reach that state of society which is so imperfectly attained by the best regulated government. But as industry is a power, and the most valuable of any, nature seems determined, suitable to her usual maxims, to bestow it on men with a very sparing hand." P. 213. And yet this writer can say, that there is not "any of mind so happy as the calm and equable." P. 259. But would not more industry and *activity* necessarily disturb this calm and happy temperament, and be apt to produce quarrels, and, consequently, more unhappiness?

" I am sceptic enough," he says, " to allow that the bad appearances, notwithstanding all my reasonings, may be compatible with such attributes as you suppose; but surely they can never prove these attributes." P. 219. But if present appearances prove *real benevolence*, I think they will go very near to prove *unbounded* benevolence, for reasons that I have alleged before, and which I shall not repeat here.

It is pretty clear to me, that Mr. Hume was not sufficiently acquainted with what has been already advanced by those who have written on the subject of the being and attributes of God. Otherwise he either would not have put such weak arguments into the mouth of his favourite *Philo*, or would have put better answers into those of his opponents. It was, I imagine, his dislike of the subject that made him overlook such writers, or give but little attention to them; and I think this conjecture concerning his aversion to the subject the better founded, from his saying, that there is a "gloom and melancholy remarkable in all devout people." P. 259.

No person really acquainted with true devotion, or those who were possessed with it, could have entertained such an opinion. What Mr. Hume had seen must have been some miserably low superstition, or wild enthusiasm, things very remote from the calm and sedate, but cheerful spirit of rational devotion.

Had he considered the nature of true devotion, he must have been sensible that the charge of gloom and melancholy can least of all apply to it. Gloom and melancholy certainly belong to the system of atheism, which entirely precludes the pleasing ideas of a benevolent Author of nature, and of a wise plan of Providence, bringing good out of all the evil we experience; which cuts off the consoling intercourse with an invisible, but omnipresent and almighty protector and friend; which admits of no settled provision for our happiness, even in this life, and closes the melancholy scene, such as Mr. Hume himself describes it, with a total annihilation.

Is it possible to draw a more gloomy and dispiriting picture of the system of the universe than Mr. Hume himself has drawn in his tenth dialogue? No melancholy religionist ever drew so dark a one. Nothing in the whole system pleases him. He finds neither *wisdom* nor *benevolence*. Speaking on the supposition of God being omnipotent and omniscient, he says, " His power we allow infinite; whatever he wills is executed; but neither man nor any other animal is happy; therefore he does not will their happiness. His wisdom is infinite; he is never mistaken in choosing the means to any end; but the course of nature tends not to human or animal felicity.; therefore it is not established for that purpose." Pp. 185, 186.

" Look round the universe," says he, " what an immense profusion of beings, animated and organized, sensible and active! You admire this prodigious variety and fecundity. But inspect a little more narrowly these living existences, the only beings worth regarding. How hostile and destructive to each other! How insufficient all of them for their own happiness! How contemptible, or odious, to the spectator! The whole presents nothing but the idea of a blind nature, impregnated by a great vivifying principle, and pouring forth from her lap, without discernment or parental care, her maimed and abortive children." Pp. 219, 220.

Compare this with the language of the pious writers of the Scriptures. " Thou art good and doest good. The Lord is good to all, and his tender mercies are over all his works. The earth is full of the goodness of the Lord. The eyes of all wait upon thee, and thou givest them their meat in due season. Thou openest thine hand, and satisfiest the desires of every living thing. The Lord reigneth: let the earth rejoice, let the inhabitants of the isles be glad thereof. Clouds and darkness are round about him; righteousness and judgment are the habitation of his throne."

In the Scriptures, the Divine Being is represented as encouraging us to cast all our care upon him who careth for us. The true Christian is exhorted to *rejoice evermore*, and especially to *rejoice in tribulation*, and persecution for righteousness' sake. Death is so far from being a frightful and disgusting thing, that he triumphs in it, and over it. *O death, where is thy sting? O grave, where is thy victory?*

Would any person hesitate about choosing to *feel* as these writers felt, or as Mr. Hume must have done? With his views of things, the calmness and composure with which, he says, he faced death, though infinitely short of the *joyful expectation* of the Christian, could not have been any thing but affectation. If, however, with his prospects, he really was as calm, placid and cheerful as he pretends, with little reason can he charge any set of *speculative principles* with a tendency to produce gloom and melancholy. If *his* system did not produce this disposition, it never can be in the power of *system* to do it.

Notwithstanding I have differed so much from Mr. Hume with respect to the principles of his treatise, we shall, in words, at least, agree in our conclusion. For though I think the being of a God, and his general benevolence and providence, to be sufficiently demonstrable, yet so many cavils may be started on the subject, and so much still remains that a rational creature must wish to be informed of concerning his maker, his duty here, and his expectations hereafter, that what Mr. Hume said by way of cover and irony, I can say with great seriousness, and I do not wish to say it much otherwise or better.

" The most natural sentiment," he says, " which a well-disposed mind will feel on this occasion, is a longing desire and expectation, that heaven would be pleased to dissipate, at least alleviate, this profound ignorance, by affording some more particular revelation to mankind, and making discoveries of the nature, attributes and operations of the divine object of our faith. A person seasoned with a just sense of the imperfections of natural reason will fly to *revealed truth* with the greatest avidity.—To be a philosophical sceptic is, in a man of letters, the first and most essential step towards being a sound believing Christian." P. 263.

I am, &c.

LETTER X.

An Examination of Mr. Hume's Essay on a Particular Providence, and a Future State.

Dear Sir,

You tell me you have been a good deal staggered with the eleventh of Mr. Hume's *Philosophical Essays*,[*] " Of a *Particular Providence* and of a *Future State*," thinking his reasoning, if not conclusive, yet so plausible, as to be well entitled to a particular reply; I shall, therefore, give it as

---

[*] " Philosophical Essays concerning Human Understanding, Ed. 2, with Additions and Corrections." 12mo. 1750.

much consideration as I flatter myself, after what I have already advanced on the same subject, you will think sufficient.

In the character of an Epicurean philosopher, addressing an Athenian audience, he says, "Allowing the gods to be the authors of the existence, or order of the universe, it follows, that they possess that precise degree of power, intelligence and benevolence which appear in their workmanship. But nothing farther can be proved, except we call in the assistance of exaggeration and flattery to supply the defects of argument and reasoning." P. 216. He farther says, "You have no reason to give *distributive justice* any particular extent, but only so far as you see it at present extend itself." P. 223.

This is the sum of his argument, which he has only repeated in his posthumous Dialogues, and the reasoning of which you will find obviated in the preceding letters. He himself makes a friend, whom he introduces as discussing the question with him, reply to it, that intelligence once proved, from our own experience and observation, we are necessarily carried beyond what we have observed to such unseen consequences as we naturally expect from such intelligence in similar cases.

"If you saw," says he, "a half-finished building, surrounded with heaps of bricks and stones, and mortar, and all the instruments of masonry, could you not infer, from the effect, that it was a work of design and contrivance; and could you not return again, from this inferred cause, to infer new additions to the effect, and conclude that the building would soon be finished, and receive all the farther improvements which art could bestow upon it?—Why then do you refuse to admit the same method of reasoning with regard to the order of nature?" &c. P. 225.

This reply appears to me to be satisfactory. But Mr. Hume refuses to acquiesce in it, on account of a supposed total *dissimilarity* between the Divine Being and other intelligent agents, and of our more perfect knowledge of man than of God. The substance of his answer is, that we know man from various of his productions, and, therefore, from this experience of his conduct, can foretell what will be the result of those of his works of which we see only a part. Whereas "the Deity," he says, "is known to us only by his productions, and is a single being in the universe, not comprehended under any species or genus, from whose experienced attributes or qualities we can, by analogy, infer any attribute or quality in him. As the universe shews wisdom and goodness, we infer wisdom and goodness. As it shews a particular degree of these perfections, we infer a particular degree of them, precisely adapted to the effects we examine. But farther attributes, and farther degrees of the same attributes, we can never be authorized to infer, or suppose, by any rules of just reasoning." Pp. 227, 228. He therefore says, " No new fact can be inferred from the religious hypothesis, no event foreseen or foretold, no reward or punishment expected or dreaded, beyond what is already known by practice and observation." P. 230.

But if the Deity be an intelligent and designing cause (of which the universe furnishes abundant evidence), he is not, in Mr. Hume's sense, an *unique*, of a genus or species by himself, but is to be placed in the general *class* of *intelligent and designing agents*, though infinitely superior to all others of that kind; so that, by Mr. Hume's own concession, we are not without some *clue* to guide us in our inquiries concerning the probable tendencies and issues of what we see.

Besides, admitting the Deity to be an *unique* with respect to intelligence, it is not with *one* of his productions only that we are acquainted. We see innumerable of them; and, as far as our experience goes, we see that all of them advance to some state of perfection. Properly speaking, nothing is left *unfinished*. It is true that particular plants and animals perish before they arrive at this state, but this is not the case with the *species;* and all individuals perish in consequence of some *general laws*, calculated for the good of the whole species, that is, of the greater part of the individuals of which it consists. Consequently, without regard to the productions of other intelligent agents, we are not destitute of *analogies*, from which to infer a future better state of things, in which there may be a fuller display of the divine attributes both of justice and benevolence.

On the whole, therefore, if we see things to be in a progress to a better state, we may reasonably conclude that the melioration will continue to proceed, and, either equably or accelerated, as we have hitherto observed it. Whatever be the *final object* of a work of design, yet, from what we know of such works, we can generally form a tolerable guess whether they be *finished* or *unfinished*, and whether any scheme be near its beginning, its middle, or its termination. We are, therefore, by no means precluded from all reasoning concerning a future state of things by the consideration of the infinite superiority of the author of the system of the universe to all other intelligent beings. Notwithstanding his superiority to any of them, he may be said to be *one of them;* and, without any information from the Scriptures, we might have discovered that in this sense, at least, *in the image of God has he made man.* Or, though God should not be considered as of the same class with any of his creatures, his productions, having the same author, supply abundance of analogies among themselves.

In the same manner, the benevolence of the Deity (which, in this place, Mr. Hume does not deny, but suppose) being simply admitted, we are at liberty to reason concerning it, as well as concerning the benevolence of any other being whatever. And therefore if, in any nearly parallel case, we can see no reason why benevolence should be limited, or why a *less* and not a *greater* degree of good should be intended, it must appear probable to us, that the greatest is intended; though, for sufficient but unknown reasons, it cannot take place at present. Just as, if we are once satisfied that any particular *parent* has a just affection for his child, we conclude that, though he does not put him into immediate possession of every thing that he has in his power to bestow upon him, it is because he is persuaded that, for the present, it would not be for his advantage; but that, in due time (of which we also naturally presume the parent himself to be the best judge) he will do much more for him, even all that his knowledge and ability can enable him to do. And though we may presume envy and jealousy to prevent this in natural parents, we cannot possibly suppose any thing of this kind to affect the *Universal Parent,* because we cannot imagine any interference of interest between this parent and his offspring.

We always argue in the same manner concerning the conduct of a *governor.* If we are once fully satisfied with respect to his *love of justice,* and have also no doubt of his *wisdom* and *power,* we immediately conclude, that every incorrigible criminal in his dominions will be properly punished; and though, for the present, many criminals walk at large, we conclude that their conduct is duly attended to, and that their future treatment will be made to correspond to it.

In like manner, if the present state of things bear the aspect of a scene of *distributive justice,* it may reasonably be considered as only the beginning of a scheme of more exact and impartial administration; so that, in due time, virtue will be more adequately rewarded, and vice more exemplarily punished, than we now see it to be. Every thing, therefore, that I have advanced on this subject in the preceding *Letters* may be perfectly well founded, notwithstanding this particular objection of Mr. Hume, and notwithstanding the great stress he lays upon it, both in this work, and in his *posthumous Dialogues*.

I am, &c.

LETTER XI.

Of the Systeme de la Nature.

DEAR SIR,

It would be tiresome to you, as well as irksome to myself, to go over *all* the atheistical writers that have been admired in their time; but there is one work much more celebrated abroad than that of Mr. Hume will probably ever be with us, that you wish me not to pass unnoticed. This is the *Systême de la Nature*.*

After what I have already observed in my six first letters, and my animadversions on Mr. Hume's Dialogues, &c. it will hardly be in my power to select any thing from this work that I have not noticed already. However, as this performance is considered by many persons as a kind of *Bible of Atheism*, and the manner in which it is written, though far from being closely argumentative, is often excellent in the mode of *declamation*, and the writer is much more bold and unreserved than Mr. Hume, I shall make such extracts as I am confident you will acknowledge contain the essence of his argument, and will be, at the same time, a pretty just specimen of the composition of the whole, with short remarks.

This writer admits of nothing but what is the object of our senses, and, in the common sense of the word, *material;* and concerning the origin of matter, and all the present laws of it, he expresses himself as follows:

" If we ask whence came matter, we say it has existed always. If we be asked whence came motion in matter, we

---

* " Système de la Nature, ou des Loix du Monde physique et du Monde moral. Par M. Mirabaud, Secretaire perpétuel, et l'un des Quarante de l'Académie Françoise." *Londres*, 1770, 2 vols. 8vo. See Vol. III. p. 214. Mirabaud died 1760, aged 86. By the following passage it appears that the *Systême* was unjustly ascribed to him: " On a mis sous le nom de cet académicien, après sa mort, un cours d'athéisme, sous le titre de *Systême de la Nature*, 1770, en 2 vol. en 8vo., qui n'est qu'un réchauffé du Spinosisme. Il est inutile d'avertir que cette insolente Philippique contre Dieu, attribuée peut-être témérairement à un académicien de Berlin, n'est pas de *Mirabaud*." Nouv. Dict. Lyons, 1804, VIII. p. 308.

answer that, for the same reason, it must have been in motion from all eternity; since motion is a necessary consequence of its existence, of its essence and its primitive properties, such as extension, gravity, impenetrability, figure, &c.* These elements, which we never find perfectly pure, being continually in action on one another, always acting and re-acting, always combining and separating, attracting and repelling, are sufficient to explain the formation of all the beings that we see. Their motions unceasingly succeed each other. They are alternately causes and effects; and thus form a vast circle of generations and destructions, combinations and decompositions, which never could have had any beginning, and can never have an end. To go higher, for the principle of action in matter, and the origin of things, is only removing the difficulty, and wholly withdrawing it from the examination of our senses."†

I will acknowledge, with this writer, that matter cannot exist without *powers*, as those of attraction, repulsion, &c. more or less modified, as in the form of gravity, elasticity, electricity, &c.; for take away all the powers, that is, all the *properties* of matter, and the substance itself vanishes from our idea. Consequently, if matter has been from eternity, these powers, and the motions which are the effects of them, must also have been from eternity. But then, in the *adjustment* of these various powers, and, consequently, in *imparting* them, there must evidently have been a knowledge, comprehension and foresight, of which the bodies possessing, and subject to those laws, are altogether incapable. I therefore conclude with certainty, that a Being superior to every thing that is the object of our senses must have imparted those powers, and have adjusted them to their proper uses; that is, that he must have *created matter itself*, which could have no existence without its powers. I am unable

---

* "Lorsqu'on demandera d'où est venu la matière? Nous dirons qu'elle a toujours existé. Si l'on demande d'où est venu le mouvement dans la matière? Nous répondrons que par la même raison elle a dû se mouvoir de toute éternité, vû que le mouvement est une suite nécessaire de son existence, de son essence et de ses propriétés primitives, telles que son étendue, sa pesanteur, son impénétrabilité, sa figure," &c. *Système*, I. p. 27.

† "Ces élémens, que nous sens ne nous montrent jamais purs, étant mis continuellement en action les uns par les autres, toujours agissant et réagissant, toujours se combinant et se séparant, s'attirant et se répoussant, suffisent pour nous expliquer la formation de tous les êtres que nous voyons; leur mouvemens naissent sans interruption les uns des autres; ils sont alternativement des causes et des effets, ils forment ainsi un vaste cercle de générations et de destructions, de combinaisons et de décompositions, qui n'a pu avoir de commencement et qui n'aura jamais de fin.— Vouloir remonter au de là pour trouver le principe de l'action dans la matière et l'origine des choses, ce n'est jamais que reculer la difficulté, et la soustraire absolument à l'examen de nos sens." *Ibid.* p. 30.

to account for what is *visible* without having recourse to a power that is *invisible;* and this invisible power I distinguish by the name of God.

"What does the word God," says he, "mean, but the impenetrable cause of the effects which astonish us, and which we cannot explain?* In this God nothing is found but a vain phantom, substituted for *the energy of nature*, which men are always determined to mistake.† Men have filled nature with spirits, because they have been almost always ignorant of true causes. For want of knowing the force of nature, they have thought it to be animated by a great spirit. For want of knowing the energy of the human machine, they have supposed that, in like manner, animated by a spirit; so that we see the word *spirit* means nothing but the unknown cause of the phenomena that we cannot explain in a natural manner."‡

To this I can only say that, if nothing that is visible *can* account for what I see, I must necessarily have recourse to something that is invisible. Just as if I hear a voice which, I am convinced, does not proceed from any thing in the room in which I am, I cannot help ascribing it to some cause without the room, unless I could believe that such a thing as *sound* could originate without any cause at all. Now men, animals, plants, and even metals and stones, are things that we can no more suppose to have existed without a cause, than a mere sound.

I am not solicitous about the term *spirit*, but I must have some name by which to distinguish that to which I ascribe such *powers* as cannot belong to any thing that I am able to see. A human body may be, and probably is, the seat of all the powers that are exerted by man; but there is in the constitution of man (of whatever materials he may consist) marks of a design and intelligence infinitely superior to any thing that is found in man. He, therefore, *must* have some superior cause, and so must every thing else that, like man, is finite. Proceeding in this manner, we must come at last to a Being whose intelligence is properly *infinite*, and then

---

* "Le mot *Dieu* ne désignera jamais que la cause inconnue des effets que les hommes ont admirés ou redoutés." *Systême*, II. p. 94.

† "Dans ce Dieu l'on ne trouvera qu'un vain phantôme, substitué à l'énergie de la nature que l'on s'est toujours obstiné à méconnoitre." *Ibid.* p. 102.

‡ "Les hommes ont rempli la nature d'*esprits*, parce qu'ils ont presque toujours ignoré les vraies causes. Faute de connoitre les forces de la nature on l'a cru animée par un *grand esprit:* faute de connoitre l'énergie de la machine humaine on l'a supposée pareillement animée par un *esprit*. D'où l'on voit que par le mot *esprit* l'on ne veut indiquer que la cause ignorée d'un phénomène qu'on ne sçait point expliquer d'une façon naturelle." *Ibid.* I. p. 102.

(besides that we are under a *necessity* of resting there) it ceases to be in the predicament of a man, or a plant, which must necessarily be dependent upon something superior to themselves; though, for that very reason, it ceases to be the object of our conceptions.

It is not properly our ignorance of the energy and secret powers of nature, that is, of what is visible in nature, that makes us ascribe them to something that we call a spirit, but rather a perfect comprehension and knowledge that such beings as we see, could not have existed without some superior cause distinct from themselves. This writer might just as well say, that it is because I am ignorant of the secret energy of nature, that I inquire for the cause of a sound that I hear, or of a watch that I meet with.

It is true that, because men cannot account for the power of thinking in themselves, they have had recourse to an invisible spirit; and, likewise, because they cannot account for the order of the universe, they have recourse to another, but greater, invisible spirit. So far the two cases resemble each other; but, in fact, they are very different. I discover the fallacy of the popular opinion concerning the supposed invisible spirit called the *soul*, or the seat of perception and thought in man, when I consider that all the phenomena of perception and thought depend upon the organization of the brain, and that therefore, whatever those powers are, they *must*, according to the received rules of philosophizing, be ascribed to that organization. We are not to multiply causes without necessity. And when I reflect farther, I see that no difficulty is, in fact, removed by ascribing the powers of perception and thought to an invisible or immaterial spirit, because there is no more perceivable connexion between what is *invisible* than what is *visible*, and those *powers*. It is true that I have no distinct idea of *any* proper seat of those mental powers, with what they can connect, or on what they may depend. But, for any thing that appears to the contrary, they may just as well connect with, and depend upon, the *brain*, as upon any invisible substance within the brain.

But when I pass from the immediate cause of thought in man to the cause of that cause, or the cause of this organization of the brain, I must necessarily look for it in something that is at least capable of understanding that organization; and this I know must be a being of intelligence infinitely superior to that of any *man*, and, therefore, certainly very different from any thing human. For the same reason it is in vain that I look for this intelligence in the earth, the sun, the moon, or the stars, or in all those bodies combined.

There is, indeed, in the universe, that kind of *unity* which bespeaks it to be *one work*, and, therefore, probably the work of one being; but we by no means see that *continuity of substance*, which we find in the brain, so as to conclude from that analogy, that the parts of the visible universe do themselves constitute a thinking substance. What is visible belonging to man *may*, for any thing we know to the contrary, be the seat of all his powers, and, therefore, according to the rules of philosophizing, which teach us not to multiply causes or substances without necessity, *must be concluded* to be so. But what is visible in the universe *cannot* be the seat of the intelligence that belongs to *it*, according to any analogy that we are acquainted with. Besides, allowing, impossible as it must be, that so disjointed a system as the material universe is, to have a *principle of thought* belonging to it, it has, however, so much the appearance of other works of design, that we must still look out for *its* author, as much as for that of a man.

Concerning the origin of the human race, this writer says, " The contemplator of nature will admit that he sees no contradiction in supposing that the human race, such as it is at present, has either been produced in time, or from all eternity. But some reflections seem to give a greater probability to the hypothesis, that man is a production in time, peculiar to the globe that we inhabit; who, consequently, has no higher origin than the globe itself, and is a result from the particular laws that govern it."* To those who, to cut the difficulty, " pretend that the human race is descended from a first man and first woman, created by the Divinity, we will say that we have some idea of *nature*, but that we have none of the *Deity* or of *creation;* and that to make use of these terms, is to say, in other words, that we are ignorant of *the energy of nature*, and that we do not know *how* it has produced the men that we see."†

* " Le contemplateur de la nature dira qu'il ne voit aucune contradiction à supposer que l'espèce humaine, telle qu'elle est aujourd'hui, a été produite soit dans le tems, soit de toute éternité.—Cependant quelques réflexions semblent favoriser ou rendre plus probable l'hypothèse que l'homme est une production faite dans le tems, particulière au globe que nous habitons, qui par conséquent ne peut dater que la formation de ce globe lui même, et qui est un résultat des loix particulières qui le dirigent." *Systême*, I. p. 82.

† " Nous dirons à ceux qui, pour trancher les difficultés, prétendent que l'espèce humaine descend d'un premier homme et d'une première femme, créés par la Divinité, que nous avons quelques idées de la nature et que nous n'en avons aucune de

It is, I acknowledge, equally reasonable to suppose the race of men to have existed from eternity without any superior cause, as to have begun to exist in time without one; but yet the latter supposition, which this writer thinks the more probable of the two, by removing the origin of man out of the obscurity of eternity, appears more glaringly absurd, being more directly opposite to every thing that we observe or experience. Had we ever seen any thing come into being in this manner, we might conclude that man *might* have done so; but having no experience of any such thing, and, on the contrary, seeing every man, animal and plant, to be descended from pre-existent parents; we necessarily conclude that every individual of the species must have come into being in this manner, till we come to the first of the species; and this first we see no difficulty in supposing to have been formed by a being of sufficient power and skill. In the same manner, we trace back a number of *echoes*, or reverberations of sound, to something that, without being itself a sound, has a power of exciting it. But the primary cause of *man* can no more be a man, than the primary cause of a *sound* can be a sound.

As this writer ascribes every thing that exists to the energy of *nature*, he seems sometimes to annex the same ideas to that word that others do to the word *God;* so that, from some passages in his work, one would imagine that he was an atheist in name only, and not in reality.

" We cannot doubt," says he, " of the power of nature to produce all the animals that we see, by the help of combinations of matter, which are in continual action."* " Nature is not a work. It has always subsisted of itself. It is in its bosom that every thing is made."† " We cannot deny but that nature is very powerful, and very industrious."‡ " Nature is not a blind cause. It does not act at random. Nothing that it does would appear *accidental* to him who should know its manner of acting, its resources and ways."§

la Divinité ni de la création, et que se servir de ces mots c'est ne dire qu'en d'autres termes que l'on ignore l'énergie de la nature et qu'on ne scait point comment elle a pu produire les hommes que nous voyons." *Ibid.* I. pp. 88, 89.

* " Nous ne pouvons douter de la puissance de la nature; elle produit tous les animaux que nous voyons à l'aide des combinaisons de la matière qui est dans une action continuelle." *Ibid.* II. pp. 153, 154.

† " *La nature n'est point un ouvrage;* elle a toujours existé par elle-même: c'est dans son sein que tout se fait." *Ibid.* II. p. 156.

‡ " Nous ne pouvons douter que la nature ne soit très puissante et très industrieuse." *Ibid.* II. pp. 157, 158.

§ La nature n'est point une cause aveugle; elle n'agit point au hazard; tout ce qu'elle fait ne seroit jamais fortuit pour celui qui connoîtroit sa façon d'agir, ses ressources et sa marche." *Ibid.* II. pp. 160, 161.

"It is nature that combines, according to certain and necessary laws, a head so organized as to make a poem. It is nature that gives a brain proper to produce such a work."* "Nature does nothing but what is necessary. It is not by accidental combinations, and random throws, that it produces the beings that we see."† "Chance is nothing but a word of imagination, like the word *God*, to cover the ignorance we are under, of the acting causes in nature, whose ways are often inexplicable."‡

If what this writer here calls *nature* be really capable of all that he ascribes to it; if it be thus powerful and industrious, if it does nothing at random, and produces beings of such intelligence as men, &c. it is indeed no bad substitute for a deity, but then it would be, in fact, only another name for the same thing. It is the *powers*, not the *substance*, that we reverence; and a power like this, capable of producing men and animals, without pre-existent parents, is a power not to be overlooked. I should even think it capable of occasioning as much superstitious dread as this writer imputes to the belief of a God. Also, if the powers of this nature favour virtue, as this writer strongly contends, it might be even apprehended that, being capable of producing men at first, it might be capable of *re-producing* them after they had been dead and buried; so that an atheist who had been very wicked, could not be quite sure of escaping the punishment of his crimes even in the grave.

But, notwithstanding all that this writer ascribes to nature, and though it does not act at random, he imagines it has no intelligence or object; which I think is not a little paradoxical. "Nature," says he, "has no intelligence or object. It acts necessarily, because it exists necessarily. It is we that have a necessary object, which is our own preservation."§ This writer, however, supposes man to act necessarily; so that merely acting *necessarily* is not incompatible

* "C'est la nature qui combine d'après des loix certaines et necessaires une tête organisée de manière à faire un poëme: c'est la nature qui lui donne un cerveau propre à enfanter un pareil ouvrage." *Ibid.* II. p. 161.
† "La nature ne fait donc rien que de nécessaire; ce n'est point par des combinaisons fortuites et par des jets hazardés qu'elle produit les êtres que nous voyons." *Ibid.* II. p. 164.
‡ "Le hazard n'est rien qu'un mot imaginé, ainsi que le mot Dieu, pour couvrir l'ignorance où l'on est des causes agissantes dans une nature dont la marche est souvent inexplicable." *Ibid.* II. p. 165.
§ "La nature n'a point de but; elle existe nécessairement; ses façons d'agir sont fixées par des loix qui découlent elles-mêmes des propriétés constitutives des êtres variés qu'elle renferme, et des circonstances que le mouvement continuel doit nécessairement amener. C'est nous qui avons un but nécessaire, c'est de nous conserver nous-mêmes." *Ibid.* II. p. 177.

with having an *object.* Consequently, nature, though acting necessarily, *may,* according to his own mode of reasoning, have an object; and that nature, or the Author of nature, *has* had various objects, is just as evident as it is that man has objects. The power that formed an *eye* had as certainly something in view, as he that constructed a *telescope.*

I am unable to pursue the inconsistencies of this celebrated writer any farther; and yet, taking the whole work together, it is the most plausible and seducing of any thing that I have yet met with in support of atheism; and the author is to be commended for writing in a frank and open manner, without the least cover or reserve, which is not the case with Mr. Hume.

I am, &c.

LETTER XII.

An Examination of some fallacious Methods of demonstrating the Being and Attributes of God.

Dear Sir,

It is, in some respects, to be regretted, that all the friends of religion do not agree in the principles on which they defend it; because it gives their common adversaries the advantage of various important concessions from some or other of them. This has, in fact, proceeded so far, that, in the opinion of some theists, the principles of professed atheists are not more dangerous than those of their particular adversaries, though equally declared theists with themselves. Also, *human passions* interfering, the enemies of atheism are apt to dispute with too much anger and rancour about their several modes of attack and defence, and to represent those who have the same ultimate object with themselves, *as favourers of atheism,* though they may hesitate to call their principles directly *atheistical.*

But, on the other hand, this very circumstance, though unfavourable in these respects, is not without some advantage; as different persons may be impressed by different modes of reasoning. And provided the great *moral purpose* be attained, which undoubtedly is an inward reverence for an invisible Being, whom we consider as the maker of us, and of all things, who is our moral governor here, and will take cognizance of our conduct hereafter, the real friends of religion, and especially those of the most truly enlarged minds, will rejoice.

Nor do we need to be alarmed at any future discovery of the weakness of any principles of religion by those who have built the most upon them. For if the superstructure itself be valued, a man will always look out for some better supports rather than let it fall altogether. There are few persons of a speculative turn of mind but must have observed this in themselves, with respect to various other valuable objects.

On how very different and opposite principles has the general doctrine of *morals* been founded, and how often have speculative persons changed their views of this seemingly momentous business? And yet it is not at all probable, that the *practice of morals* has ever suffered from this cause. On what different principles, also, have the civil and religious rights of men been founded, by persons who have been equally ready to lay down their lives in defence of them, and who change their speculative opinions without becoming advocates for slavery?

Why then should any friend of religion be alarmed because one person thinks that the being of God, and the great truths of natural religion, are to be proved in one way, and another person in a different way? If, as we must all acknowledge, it would be most injurious to call any person an atheist, merely because he could not prove the being of a God at all, much more, certainly, must it be injurious to call a person an atheist who does it satisfactorily to himself, though not so to us.

It is very rarely that thinking and speculative persons are convinced of any mistake of consequence; but let the confutation be ever so clear and undeniable, if the disputant be a man of virtue, I should not be apprehensive that even principles the most indisputably (yet, in fact, only *consequentially*) atheistical would ever make him an atheist.

What would become of the advocates of the doctrine of the *Trinity*, if those only should be allowed to be Trinitarians, who explained and defended it in the same manner? To say nothing of the general difference between ancient and modern times in that respect, few societies, I apprehend, of that denomination of Christians at this day, would, on this principle, hold communion with each other.

In general, the truth of any particular proposition may be so firmly assented to, and may be so intimately connected with, numberless other tenets, that a man's *whole system of opinions* must give way before that one doctrine can be rooted out of his mind; and so total a revolution in the principles of men, who really think at all for themselves, so seldom happens, that it is no reasonable object of apprehension. It is happy for us that we are so constituted. Without this, we should be in a state of endless fluctuation; and it is almost better to have any principles, and any character, than no fixed principles, no proper character at all.

With respect to the subject of these letters, I shall hope to derive this advantage from the discussion, that those persons who are atheistically inclined, and who have been confirmed in their disbelief of the principles of religion by the injudicious manner in which some of its friends have defended it, may find their triumph premature; and that the system of theism is not overturned, though they should have succeeded in their refutation of some principles which have been *imagined* to be essential to it, and necessary supports of it.

With this calm, and I hope just view of the subject, I shall, in this letter, endeavour to explain the fallacy of some of the speculative principles on which real friends of religion have, at different times, endeavoured to support the doctrines of a God and of a Providence. And, in doing this, I shall have no fear of increasing, but, on the contrary, some hope of lessening, the number of atheists.

1. I shall not detain you long with the opinion of those who maintain that the belief of a God is an *instinctive principle;* because I presume it will, at this day, be generally acknowledged, that there is no evidence of *any* idea, or principle, being properly instinctive or *innate*. We come into the world furnished with proper senses to receive the various impressions to which we are exposed; and the traces in the mind, left by those impressions, appear to be the elements of all the ideas, and all the knowledge we ever acquire. Being then possessed of a natural capacity of acquiring to a certain degree every kind of valuable knowledge, and the knowledge of God and of religion, as well as of other things, it is not agreeable to the analogy of nature to have the same things impressed upon us in another, and quite different manner.

Besides, had the idea of God been originally impressed upon the minds of all men, the character would, no doubt, have been the same, and would not have been liable to so great variation, and perversion, as we find it to have been. Nor could we imagine it could have been so nearly, if not entirely effaced, as it appears to have been in some whole nations; if, indeed, it can be suppossed possible, on that hypothesis, for *any* person to have been an atheist. This very unphilosophical opinion, that the belief of a God is an instinctive principle, not to be deduced by reasoning from any appearances in nature, has, however, been asserted very lately, and every other mode of defending the primary truths of religion has been most arrogantly exploded and ridiculed, by Dr. Beattie and Dr. Oswald, on principles before advanced by Dr. Reid; and yet of the good *intentions* of these writers, in this singular conduct, I never entertained a doubt, though such absurd principles, so haughtily advanced, and so weakly supported, in this enlightened age, deserve, in my opinion, every other censure. See my *Examination of these Writers*. (Vol. III.)

2. Descartes thought that the very *idea* of a God was a sufficient proof of his existence. This opinion, if defensible at all, implies the former. For unless the idea of God be of such a nature as that it could not have been acquired by any impressions to which we are exposed, it must be impossible to say but that it may have been so formed. What is there in our idea of God but human perfections magnified; and what is our idea of *infinity* itself, but the mere negation of bounds?

3. There is another mode of reasoning concerning the being of God, which, I believe, originated with Dr. Clarke, and is, I imagine, peculiar to this country, but it does not appear ever to have given general satisfaction; though some very eminent metaphysicians are still strongly attached to it. To me, however, the fallacy of it seems very obvious.

According to this author, there must be a God, or an original designing cause of all things, because it would be as much a contradiction to suppose the contrary, as to suppose that *two and two* are not equal to *four*. He also says, that the idea of God cannot be excluded from the mind, any more than the ideas of *space* or *duration*, though we use every effort we can for that purpose.

Now a *contradiction* is saying and unsaying, affirming and denying a thing at the same time, or in the same sentence; so that there is a manifest *contrariety*, or *incompatibility*, between those ideas that are asserted to coincide; and this must appear without any reasoning on the subject, just as if we should say *white is black*, and yet retain the ideas usually annexed to those terms. We immediately perceive, without any reasoning, that *black* cannot be *white*, or *white*, *black*. If we say that *two and two* are *five*, it is a contradiction, though in form one step short of a *direct* one. To make it a direct contradiction, we should first say that *two and two* are *four*, and then that *four* is *five*, which only is a direct, or proper contradiction.

Now where is the proper contradiction, direct or indirect, in saying *there is no God?* If we reduce it to a formal proposition, it is, *the universe exists without a cause.* Now, false as the proposition is, it is no more a contradiction (i. e. *in terms*, and there is no other proper contradiction) than to say that *God exists without a cause*, which is a truth. Because neither is the idea, annexed to the term *universe*, the direct reverse of the idea annexed to the term *uncaused*, nor does the idea annexed to the term *God* coincide with it.

As to the impossibility of excluding from our minds the idea of a Deity, it is altogether an affair of *consciousness;* and with respect to myself, I have no scruple to say, that I find no difficulty at all in excluding the ideas of every thing in nature, except those of *space* and *duration*, and I cannot help being surprised that the contrary should ever have been asserted.

It is true that the belief of what actually exists compels us to the belief of a God, or an uncaused being, different from mere space. But exclusive of the consideration of *an existing universe*, from which I infer the belief of a God, as the necessary cause of it, there is nothing in the mere *idea* of a Deity (as there evidently is in the idea of space) that prevents a possibility of its being excluded from the mind. But it is proper that so respectable a writer as Dr. Clarke should be heard in his own words.

" The only true idea of a self-existent, or necessarily existing Being, is the idea of a being, the supposition of whose non-existing is an express contradiction. The relation of equality between *twice two* and *four* is an absolute necessity, only because it is an immediate contradiction in terms to suppose them unequal. This is the only idea we can frame of an absolute necessity ; and to use the word in any other sense, seems to be using it without any signification at all. If any one now ask what sort of idea, the idea of that Being is, the supposition of whose non-existing is thus an express contradiction, I answer, it is the first and simplest idea we can possibly frame,—which (unless we forbear thinking at all) we cannot possibly extirpate, or remove out of our minds, of a most simple Being, absolutely eternal and infinite, original and independent."* Yet, as I have said before, I cannot imagine any difficulty in excluding this idea. But he argues the same thing in a different manner.

" That he who supposes there may possibly be no eternal and infinite Being in the universe, supposes likewise a contradiction, is evident from hence,—that when he has done his utmost in endeavouring to imagine that no such being exists, he cannot avoid imagining *an eternal and infinite nothing;* that is, he will imagine eternity and immensity removed out of the universe, yet that, at the same time, they still continue there." P. 18.

Here I think is a manifest fallacy. If, by an *eternal and infinite nothing*, he meant that nothing will be eternal and infinite but *space*, it is *false*, but surely no *contradiction;* and though an eternal and infinite Deity be removed, an eternal and infinite space will not. If there be no reference to the idea of space (which, indeed, is not mentioned), the inconclusiveness of the argument is too obvious to have escaped the observation of any person.

I acknowledge, with Dr. Clarke, that a finite being cannot be self-existent; but I do not feel the force of his reasoning on the subject, because it is the same with the preceding. " To suppose a finite being to be self-existent, is to say, that it is a contradiction for that being not to exist, the absence of which may yet be conceived without a contradiction, which is the greatest absurdity in the world." P. 44. Here he takes it for granted, that the idea of the self-existence of any being implies its being a contradiction for that being not to exist.

But though Dr. Clarke advances thus far *a priori*, that is, without any reference to an *existing universe*, in proof of the being of a God, he does not pretend to prove the divine *intelligence* in this manner, nor yet his *power*. " That the self-existent Being, is—an *understanding*, and really *active* being, does not indeed appear to us by considerations *a priori*, because—we know not wherein *intelligence* consists, nor can we see the immediate and necessary connexion of it with *self-existence*." P. 51. " The self-existent Being, the supreme cause of all things, must of necessity have infinite power," because " all things in the universe were made by him, and are entirely dependent upon him; and all the powers of all things are derived from him." P. 73.

But, what is more extraordinary, this writer thinks he can

* Demonstration, &c. Ed. 8, p. 17.

prove the *moral attributes of God* from his intelligence only. This, however, considering that he does not pretend to prove intelligence itself *a priori*, is not, strictly speaking, an argument *a priori*.

That " the supreme Cause and Author of all things must of necessity be a being of infinite goodness, justice and truth, and all other moral perfections," he proves from this consideration, that a being of infinite intelligence must perceive those *necessary fitnesses of things*, on which, according to him, morality depends ; and, " having no want of any thing, it is impossible his will should be influenced by any wrong affection," and, therefore, " he must of necessity—do always what he knows to be fittest to be done, i. e. he must act always according to the strictest rules of infinite goodness, justice and truth, and all other moral perfections." Pp. 114—116.

As the idea concerning the *foundation of morals*, on which this argument proceeds, is another subject of discussion, I shall not enter into it here, except just observing, that I perceive no necessary connexion between *intelligence*, as such, and any particular *intention* or *object* whatever ; and, therefore, nothing can prove actual *benevolence*, in preference to *malevolence*, but the actual production of *happiness*, in preference to *misery*, or, at least, a manifest tendency to it, in what is actually produced.

Dr. Clarke's mode of reasoning is not very different from that of Descartes and others, who maintain that we can prove the existence of a self-existent being from the very *idea* we have of it. That the reader may see how he distinguishes in this case, I shall just recite what he says on the subject.

" I must have an idea of something actually existing without me, and I must see wherein consists the absolute impossibility of removing that idea, and consequently of supposing the non-existence of the thing, before I can be satisfied, from that idea, that the thing actually exists. The bare having an idea of the proposition, *there is a self-existent being*, proves, indeed, the thing not to be impossible (for of an impossible proposition there is properly no idea), but that it actually *is* cannot be proved from the idea, unless the certainty of the *actual existence* of a necessarily existing being follows from the *possibility* of the existence of such a being ; which that it does, in this particular case, many learned men have indeed thought, and their subtle arguings upon this head are sufficient to raise a cloud not very easy to be seen through. But it is a much clearer and more convincing

way of arguing, to demonstrate, that there does actually exist without us a being whose existence is necessary and of itself, by shewing the evident contradiction contained in the contrary supposition,—and, at the same time, the absolute impossibility of destroying or removing some ideas, as of eternity and immensity, which, therefore, must needs be modes or attributes of a necessary being actually existing."
P. 21.

Since, however, *mere space*, as I have observed before, may easily be conceived to have existed *infinite* and *eternal*, without any thing to occupy it, it certainly cannot be necessary to suppose it the attribute of any other being. This is manifestly very unlike the case of *black*, *white*, *long*, *broad*, or other *mere properties*, which cannot be conceived without some *subject* to which they belong. The dispute whether space be a *substance*, or a *property*, is, in fact, merely, or little more than verbal ; because we know nothing of any thing but its properties. But if *a capacity of subsisting, in idea, by itself* be a characteristic of *substance*, as opposed to *property*, space, undoubtedly, ought to be denominated a substance, and not a mere property ; though, when occupied by any other substance, it may assume the appearance of a property belonging to that substance. For, take away the substance, and the space it occupied will not, in idea, go with it. Nay, in that sense, it is more of the nature of substance than any thing else, because it is impossible, even in idea, to suppose it not to be permanent.

If the whole of what Dr. Clarke has advanced, on the proof of the being of a God, be attentively considered, it will not be very easy to say what his idea of God, as proved *a priori*, is. It is that of a being self-existent, eternal, and co-extended with infinite space, but not space. It is the cause of all things, but without *power, intelligence*, or *moral attributes;* for these he makes to depend upon the perceived relation of things. Consequently, they pre-suppose intelligence, which he acknowledges cannot be proved *a priori*.

In fact, therefore, he proves nothing *a priori* but *mere being*, without any proper *powers* whatever. But the terms, *being* or *substance*, give no ideas at all when divested of powers or properties. So that, in reality, notwithstanding his assertion of the contrary, it is nothing but *empty space* that he is capable of proving *a priori*. And, with respect to this, I perfectly agree with him, because, do what we will, we cannot so much as *suppose* infinite and eternal space not to have existed.

Far, however, am I from saying that a Deity, an *efficient Deity*, with all his attributes, is not, properly speaking, *necessarily existent*, or that his existence is not, in reality, as necessary as that of space itself. But then we come to the knowledge of this necessity, with respect to him, in a different manner. It is by beginning *a posteriori*, finding that, in consequence of the *actual existence* of beings that must have had a cause, there must have been some being that could not have had a cause, though we are altogether at a loss to conceive, *a priori*, *how* or *why* he should exist without a cause, and can, in idea, easily imagine him not to have existed, which is not the case with respect to space. Then, the necessary existence of a supreme cause once supposed, there are various attributes, as those of *eternity*, *immensity* and *unity*, that may either with certainty, or with the greatest probability, be deduced from the consideration of *necessary existence*.

But though to us, and our conceptions, there be this difference between the idea of the existence of space, and of that of the Deity, there may not be any in reality. Indeed, the Deity could not have been *necessarily existent*, if there had not been, in the nature of things, if we may use the phrase, (which, however, can only be improperly applied in this case,) as much reason for his existence, as for that of space. But neither the term *reason*, nor any thing equivalent to it, ought, in strictness, to be used in this case, lest it should imply, contrary to the supposition, that there is some proper *cause* of the divine existence; whereas, he cannot have had any cause.

On this account, I dislike the phraseology of Dr. Clarke, when he sometimes speaks of *necessity being the cause of the divine existence*. Indeed, the whole of our language is so appropriated to *finite* and *caused* beings, that it is hardly possible to use any part of it in speaking with strict propriety of a Being *infinite* and *uncaused*. We should, therefore, forgive one another any oversights of this nature that we inadvertently fall into.

I am, &c.

LETTER XIII.

Of the Ideas of Cause *and* Effect, *and the Influence of Mr. Hume's Opinion on this Subject, in the Argument for the Being of a* God.

Dear Sir,

As some persons have imagined that the cause of atheism has derived considerable advantage from Mr. Hume's ideas concerning the nature of *cause and effect*, I shall, in this letter, endeavour to shew that the apprehension is without foundation.

Mr. Hume says, that all we can pretend to know concerning the connexion of cause and effect, is their constant *conjunction;* by the observance of which the mind is necessarily led from the one to the other. From this the friends of religion have supposed that if this representation be just, the connexion is merely *arbitrary*, and, therefore, that such things as we have usually called *effects may* take place without any thing that we have usually observed to correspond to them, as their *causes.* Consequently, that, for any thing that we know to the contrary, the universe itself may have existed from eternity without any superior cause.

To guard against this, some of the friends of religion deny that our idea of *power* or *causation* is derived from any thing that we properly observe. But, imperfect as Mr. Hume's ideas on the subject are, (notwithstanding his laborious and tiresome discussion of it, and its being evidently a favourite topic with him,) I think I have sufficiently shewn in the third of the *Essays* prefixed to my edition of *Hartley's Theory of the Mind,* (Vol. III. p. 189,) that there is nothing in the idea of *power* or *causation,* (which is only the same idea differently modified,) that is not derived from the impressions to which we have been subject, this being to be ranked in the class of *abstract ideas,* where it does not appear that Mr. Hume ever thought of looking for it. In the Essay I here refer to, p. 191, I have shewn that the idea of *power* is far from being, what some take it to be, a simple idea, but that, on the contrary, it is one of the most complex ideas that we have, consisting of what is common to numberless impressions of very different kinds.

Besides, if the idea of power be any thing that cannot be acquired by *experience,* it comes under the description of other *innate principles* or *ideas*, which have been so long, and, I think, so justly exploded, that I think myself at liberty to take it for granted that there is no such thing.

But I shall proceed to observe that, in whatever manner we come by the idea of power or causation, it is an idea that all men have, and corresponds to something *real* in the relation of the things that suggest it. It is true that all we properly *see* of a *magnet*, and a *piece of iron*, is that, at certain distances, they approach to one another, and of a *stone*, that, in certain circumstances, it invariably tends towards the earth, and we cannot give any proper or satisfactory *reason* why either of these effects should take place in these circumstances. Yet we have always found that in a similar constant conjunction of appearances, we have never failed to discover, whenever we have been able to make any discovery at all, that the event could not have been otherwise. And though, in these cases, we have only discovered a *nearer*, and never the *ultimate* cause of any appearance, yet there is an invariable experience in favour of *some* real and sufficient cause in all such conjunctions.

In consequence of this experience, it is indelibly impressed upon the minds of all men, that all events whatever, and all productions whatever, must have a necessary and adequate cause, so that nothing can begin to be without a cause foreign to itself. And let any person pretend what he will, he must himself (in consequence of the impressions to which he, together with the rest of mankind, has uniformly been exposed) have come under the influence of it, and of course, have the same persuasion.

Though, therefore, by means of some secret bias, and sophistical argumentation, a man may come to be persuaded that the universe has had no superior cause, he cannot deny but that all other things, (which the theist must shew to be in the same predicament with the universe,) must have had such a cause, so that nothing is to be apprehended from his idea of *the nature of causation in general.* Whatever that idea be, (and, in fact, it will be the same with that of the rest of mankind, let any person give whatever account of it he pleases,) he will necessarily expect a superior cause in those circumstances in which mankind in general will be satisfied that a cause is requisite.

Different persons *feel*, and are *persuaded* differently enough in some cases; but where the influences, to which their minds have been subject, have necessarily been nearly the same, the impressions made on them cannot be materially different. In this case, I should sooner imagine that the ideas annexed to the words *hunger* and *thirst*, should be different in different persons, than the ideas annexed to the words *power* and *causation*, or that they should have different effects in their serious argumentations.

I am, &c.

LETTER XIV.
An Examination of Mr. Hume's Metaphysical Writings.

Dear Sir,

You are surprised, you tell me, that Mr. Hume, so great a master of reasoning, so cool and dispassionate a writer, and so subtle a metaphysician, should have written so loosely and unguardedly, as you are now convinced he has done in this *posthumous work* of his, a work of which, it is evident, he made great account, by his taking such effectual measures for its publication after his death. But you cannot well suppose, having always entertained a different idea, that I can be sufficiently well-founded in the censure I have passed on his *metaphysical writings in general* in my ninth letter, and, therefore, you wish I would enter on the proof of what I have advanced, by a distinct exhibition of *all* that Mr. Hume has done in this way; that when all the observations he has advanced shall be seen without the imposition of his style and manner, its real merit, its solidity or futility, may plainly appear.

Now I am ready to give the fullest satisfaction on this subject, and I should not have ventured to throw out that *general censure*, without being prepared to justify it in all the particulars, if you should call upon me to do it. Besides, I am not without hopes, that when you see on how narrow a foundation Mr. Hume's fame as a metaphysician stands, his authority as a *reasoner* will not weigh, so much as it has hitherto done, with you and others who have only a general and indistinct notion of his being *a great philosopher*, and an acute and guarded writer. This I shall do in as succinct a manner as I can, in a regular analysis of all his *Essays* that are in the least to our present purpose.

In the first of his *Philosophical Essays*, " Of the different Species of Philosophy," which is only an introduction to the rest, it appears that he had no idea of the connexion of the different faculties of the mind, and their dependence upon one principle, as that of *association.* For he says, " The mind is endowed with several powers and faculties," and " these powers are totally distinct from each other." P. 14. But we may " hope that philosophy—may carry its researches still farther, and discover, at least, in some degree, the secret springs and principles by which the human mind is actuated in its operations." P. 15. He says, however, " it is probable that one operation and principle of the mind depends on another, which again may be resolved into one more general and universal." P. 16. What that principle is, it is evident Mr. Hume had no idea.

In his second Essay, " Of the Origin of our Ideas," I find nothing that could have been *new,* but an ill-founded suspicion, " that the simple ideas are not always, in every instance, derived from the corresponding impressions," p. 27 ; merely because, having had ideas from actual impression of the extremes of any particular *colour,* we are able, without any farther assistance from actual impressions, to raise the idea of the intermediate shades of the same colour ; not considering that this amounts to nothing more than a difference of *greater* or *less,* and, therefore, is not properly any new idea at all. It is no more than forming an idea of a middle sized hill, after having seen small hillocks and large mountains.

Let a tender eye be strongly impressed with a luminous object of white, or any other colour, and if the eye be immediately shut, the impression will of itself change into various other colours, as well as shades of the same colour ; and there can be no doubt but that this would have been the case originally, though no such colours had been known before. Now the substance of the brain being the same with that of the *retina,* and of the other nerves, it must be capable of such changes of affection as these, from causes within itself, but still the necessary consequence of external impressions.

In the third Essay, he reduces all the cases *of the connexion* or association *of ideas* to three, viz. *resemblance, contiguity* in place or time, and *cause and effect,* without attempting at a conjecture how ideas, thus related to each other, come to be associated, or what circumstances they have in common ; though it was so easy to perceive that in all of them, the immediate cause is nothing more or less than *joint impression ;* the universal and simple law of association being this, that two sensations or ideas present to the mind at the same time, will afterwards recall each other, which was well understood by Mr. Locke, and all who had treated of association before Mr. Hume. Let us now see how easily this observation will explain Mr Hume's three cases.

Things connected in *time* and *place* are generally considered together, or so near to each other, that the remains of one of the ideas is not gone out of the mind before the other has entered it. This is the reason why we so readily repeat numbers in their progressive order, and are not so well able to do it in a retrograde order. We have been most accustomed to repeat them in that order.

Resemblance is a *partial sameness*, and when that part of any idea which is the very same with part of another, is excited, it is evidently in consequence of a former joint impression that the remainder of the same idea is revived also.

Mr. Hume says, that *contrariety* may perhaps be considered as a species of *resemblance*, for a reason for which I must refer the reader to the Essay itself.* But things opposed to one another are frequently *compared* and *considered together*. It is, therefore, from frequent joint impression that their easy association is most naturally to be accounted for.

Things that are *causes and effects* to each other are also often contemplated together, and by habit we do not consider our knowledge of any thing to be complete, without knowing the cause, if it be an effect, or the effect, if it be a cause. We think the idea to be as incomplete as that of the head of a man without his body, or of his body without his head. We feel them as different parts of the same thing.

Little and imperfect, as what Mr. Hume has advanced on this subject manifestly is, he seems to have imagined that he had done something very great, when he concludes the Essay with saying, " the full explication of this principle, and all its consequences, would lead us into reasonings too profound and too copious for these Essays. It is sufficient at present to have established this conclusion, that the three connecting principles of all ideas are the relations of resemblance, contiguity and causation." P. 46.

---

* " Contrast or contrariety is a species of connexion among ideas, which may, perhaps, be considered as a species of resemblance. Where two objects are contrary, the one destroys the other, i. e. is the cause of its annihilation; and the idea of annihilation of an object implies the idea of its former existence." Essay III. p. 44. *Note.*

The fourth Essay, entitled "Sceptical Doubts," relates to our inferring an effect from a cause, asserting, that it is by a process that is not properly *reasoning*, because all that we observe is the two separate ideas, and we are altogether ignorant of their connexion; and in his fifth Essay, entitled, quaintly enough, "Sceptical Solution of these Doubts," he says, p. 73, that we make the inference by the *principle* of "Custom or Habit," which comes to this, that the two ideas have always been associated together, so that, as he expresses it, the mind is naturally led from one of them to the other, or, as he should have said more properly, one of them will necessarily introduce the other.

Leaving the question in this state, he may, with superficial readers, have weakened the foundation of our reasoning from effects to causes, as if it was properly no *reasoning* at all (which is language that he frequently uses), but only an arbitrary, and perhaps ill-founded, association of ideas. Whereas he would only have done justice to his subject, to have added, that, having found, in all such *constant* conjunctions of ideas, with respect to which we have been able to make any discovery at all, that the conjunction was really *necessary*, we conclude that the conjunction, if constant, is equally necessary, even when we are not able distinctly to perceive it. We, therefore, *presume* it, and securely act upon it. Indeed, without having made any discovery at all, we could not but be sensible, that if two events always follow one another, there must be some sufficient reason for it.

As almost every pretension to *discovery*, or *novelty*, is contained in this observation of Mr. Hume's, I shall consider it a little more strictly. When we say that two events, or appearances, are *necessarily connected*, all that we can mean is, that some more general law of nature must be violated before those events can be separated. For example, I find that the sounding of one musical string will make another string that is in unison, &c. with it, to sound also; and finding this observation invariable, I call the sounding of the first string the *cause*, and that of the second the *effect*, and have no apprehension of being disappointed in my expectation of the consequence. But I do not see what should make this conjunction necessary, till I discover that sound consists of a vibratory motion of the air, and that the air being put into this vibratory motion by the first string, communicates the same to the second by its pulses, in the same manner as the first string itself was made to vibrate.

In like manner, it was always known (and mankind have always acted on the persuasion) that respiration is necessary to animal life, and that air frequently breathed, &c. is fatal to it, though it is only of late that we have discovered the connexion of those effects with the cause. In due time we may discover the cause of this cause, &c.

The idea annexed to the term *cause* or *necessary agency*, is not a simple idea, or what could originally have been formed in the mind by the perception of any two other ideas, as Mr. Hume seems to have expected (and which notion alone could suggest any difficulty in the case), but it represents the impression left in the mind by observing what is common to numberless cases in which there is a constant conjunction of appearances or events, in some of which we are able to see the proximate cause of the conjunction, but with respect to the rest we only *presume* it from the similarity of the cases. Notwithstanding, therefore, a definite idea, corresponding to the words *cause*, or *power*, does not occur to the mind on the original comparison of any two particular ideas, the inference from effects to causes, whether Mr. Hume will call it *reasoning* or not, is, in many cases, as safe as any reasoning whatever, so that no sceptic can derive the least advantage from this consideration.

The latter part of this Essay (which I dare say Mr. Hume considered as the first in importance in the whole work) contains a very imperfect and manifestly false account of the difference between *belief* and *imagination.* " Belief," he says, " is nothing but a more vivid, lively, forceable, firm, steady conception of an object, than what the imagination alone is ever able to attain." P. 82. And to account for this *manner* of conception, he says, that whenever we are led from one idea to another, by the connexion of *resemblance* or *contiguity*, and therefore, probably, by that of *causation* too, we at the same get a *stronger* conception of it than we should otherwise attain. Unable to account for this, he ascribes the fact to an *instinct of nature.* But he might just as well have done what Drs. Reid, Beattie and Oswald, did afterwards, viz. ascribe the sentiment of *belief itself*, as well as that which is the *cause of belief* to an arbitrary instinct of nature.

In reality, nothing can be more evidently false than what

he here supposes. For how often does it happen that we are more affected by a representation of fictitious distress, in a novel, or on the theatre, than by instances of real distress in common life? It is true that, *cæteris paribus*, *reality* makes a stronger impression than *fiction*; and, therefore, when an impression is, by artificial means, made stronger than usual, it sometimes imposes upon us for truth. But the idea annexed to the word *truth* is of a very complex nature, and is the impression that is left in the mind by thousands of cases in which *real existence* has been discriminated from that which has none.

A child hears a tale of distress, and having always had the truth told him, he, of course, believes it, and, according to his previously acquired sensibility, is affected with it; but he inquires farther, and finds that he has been imposed upon. Either no such person existed, or such and such things did not happen to him. He also reads tales of distress, &c. in books, but finds, by comparing them with other books, and other accounts, that they had no existence. From much observation of this kind, a complex idea, formed by a number of circumstances, is left in the mind, and to this he gives the name of *truth*, an idea which he learns to respect more and more every day, and which he acquires a habit of affixing, with all its *secondary ideas* of respect, with justness and effect, as he advances in life; so that, independently of the *strength of our feelings*, or imagination, we act very differently, according as we see reason to annex this idea of *truth* to a story, or not.

Mr. Hume says, " When a sword is levelled at my breast, does not the idea of wounds and pain strike me more strongly than when a glass of wine is presented to me, even though, by accident, this idea should occur after the appearance of the latter object?" P. 90. But let an executioner, whom he believes to have a commission to run a sword through his body, be at the distance of a hundred miles from him, and though there be neither a sword, nor the figure of a sword, near him, he would, I doubt not, by only *thinking* of a sword, in those circumstances, feel very differently, and more strongly, than if he should take a real sword in his own hand, and hold the point of it to his naked breast, when he had no apprehension of any design to hurt himself with it. But how does this tally with Mr. Hume's account of the difference between belief and fiction?

It is evident that Mr. Hume had no idea of the extent

of the power of association in the human mind, by means of which a single idea may consist of thousands of parts, being a miniature of numberless *trains of ideas*, and of whole successive *states of mind*, and yet be perfectly distinct from other ideas, consisting of as many parts, every such complex idea retaining its separate character and powers. The very *names* of persons famous in history excite in our minds an epitome of all that we know concerning them, the particulars of which we may have forgotten. How complex also are the ideas belonging to words expressive of *national customs, ranks* and *orders of men*, which, however, when pronounced ever so slightly, excite ideas perfectly distinct from each other, as much as those denoting the most simple ideas.

Now the ideas of *cause, effect, reason, instinct, probability, contingency, truth, falsehood,* &c. &c. &c. are of this nature, requiring definitions of some extent; and the ideas they in fact excite are miniatures of much more than enters into the shortest possible description of them; for they were not attained in that manner; and yet all the parts perfectly coalesce, and form distinct and permanent ideas. I have endeavoured to give some account of this business in the third of the *Essays* prefixed to my edition of *Hartley's Theory of the Mind.* (Vol. III. p. 189.)

Mr. Hume, in his sixth Essay, "Of Probability," says, that the "concurrence of several views in a particular event begets immediately, by an inexplicable contrivance of nature, the sentiment of belief." P. 94. "Let any one try," he says, "to account for this operation of the mind upon any of the received systems of philosophy, and he will be sensible of the difficulty." P. 97. On the system of Hartley there is no difficulty in it at all.

In the seventh Essay, "Of the Idea of Power," he only more particularly insists upon it, that we know of no connexion between the idea of any cause and that of any effect, though we suppose there *is* some connexion. Of this I have given, I presume, a sufficient account already.

In his eighth Essay "Of Liberty and Necessity," he very clearly illustrates some of the arguments in favour of Necessity; but not having any comprehension of the *great system*, of which that doctrine is a part, he, without the least reason, and without the least concern, abandons it to the most shocking immoral consequences.* Whereas, in rea-

---

* Such, however, as a *Necessarian*, expecting no future retribution, can scarcely refuse to admit. See *Essay* VIII., the Second *Objection*, and the *Answer*, pp. 159, 162.

lity, nothing is more favourable to the most sublime sentiments of virtue, in all its branches, as I have shewn at large in my *Illustrations of that doctrine.*

His ninth Essay, "Of the Reason of Animals," contains very little indeed. He only asserts, that "it is custom alone which engages animals, from every object that strikes their senses, to infer its usual attendant, and carries their imaginations from the appearance of the one, to conceive the other, in that strong and lively manner which we denominate belief." P. 169. This, unable to give any better account of, he calls *instinct*, and says, that man avoids fire by instinct also. Whereas, if by instinct be meant any thing different from the association of ideas (which certainly were not born with us), nothing is more contrary to fact. A child knows nothing of a dread of fire, but acquires it in consequence of the sensation of pain from it. He can even hardly be prevented from putting his finger into the flame of a candle. How Mr. Hume could reconcile this well-known fact with a proper *instinctive dread of fire*, is not easy to say.

The tenth Essay, "Of Miracles," is intended to support a principle, according to which the relation of no appearance whatever, not evidently similar to former appearances, can be credible; a principle which we see refuted every day in experimental philosophy, and which nothing could have given the least countenance to, or have entitled to any consideration, but its affecting the credit of the miracles recorded in the Scriptures. On this account it has been refuted by many persons, and I have considered it in my "Institutes of Natural and Revealed Religion." (Vol. II. pp. 114—116.)

The eleventh Essay, "Of a Particular Providence and of a Future State," I have examined in my tenth Letter.

In his twelfth Essay, "Of the Academical or Sceptical Philosophy," Mr. Hume maintains that, because all we know of any object is the idea of it in our minds, we can never prove, that those ideas, or perceptions, "could not arise from the energy of the mind itself, or from the suggestion of some invisible and unknown spirit, or from some other cause still more unknown to us." P. 241. And that the supposition of a connexion between those perceptions of the mind and external objects is without any foundation in reasoning; not considering that we have just the same reason for believing the existence of external objects, that we have for the truth of the Copernican system. They are the easiest hypotheses for acknowledged facts, as I have shewn at large in the Introduction to my *Examination of the Writings of Drs. Reid, Beattie* and *Oswald.* (Vol. III. pp. 22—24.)

His observation, p. 243, that *all sensible qualities,* (and, therefore, *extension* itself,) are in the mind, and not without us, is trifling. He might as well have said, that because *sound* is a thing formed within a musical instrument, and not without it, there is nothing without it that produces the sound.

To his objection to the infinite divisibility of matter, p. 246, to some angles being infinitely less than others, and those again divisible *ad infinitum,* which he allows to be *demonstrable,* and yet says, is *big with contradiction and absurdity,* at the same time that he acknowledges that " nothing can be more sceptical, or more full of doubt and hesitation, than this scepticism itself," I surely need say nothing. This does not amount to so much as a *sceptical solution of a sceptical doubt.* It may rather be called *the sceptical proposal of a sceptical doubt.*

In the conclusion of this last Essay, we find the outline of all the scepticism of his posthumous work, with the same paltry *cover,* viz. that " all reasoning from the relation of cause and effect" is founded on " a certain instinct of our nature, which—may be fallacious and deceitful." P. 251. That we can never " satisfy ourselves concerning any determination we may form with regard to the origin of worlds, and the situation of nature from and to eternity." P. 255. That "divinity or theology, as it proves the existence of a Deity, &c., has a foundation in reason, so far as it is supported by experience," (which support in a former Essay he absolutely denies it to have,) "but its best and most solid foundation is *faith* and divine revelation." P. 259.

In the first of these Essays, Mr. Hume had said, " We have, in the following Essays, attempted to throw some light upon subjects, from which uncertainty has hitherto deterred the wise, and obscurity the ignorant." P. 18. How very small is the light that he has thrown, and mixed with how much darkness, I need not repeat. " Happy," says he, " if we can unite the different species of philosophy, by reconciling profound inquiry with clearness, and truth with novelty; and still more happy, if, reasoning in this easy manner, we can undermine the foundations of an abstruse philosophy, which seems to have served hitherto only as a shelter to superstition, and a cover to absurdity and error." Pp. 18, 19.

Now, I neither see the *profundity* nor the *clearness* of his reasoning, except in things with respect to which he is far from being *original*, notwithstanding his advantage of a command of language and a great power of perspicuity, where his argument would admit of it. As to the *abstruse philosophy* which he meant to undermine, it could be nothing but the doctrine of *certainty*, and a steady persuasion concerning *truth*, and especially the truths of natural and revealed religion ; and what kind of a mind must that man have had, to whom *this* could give any satisfaction!

All men by no means judge of the value of publications by the same rules with Mr. Hume, or perhaps his own Essays would be in more danger than he himself imagined. " When we run over libraries, persuaded of these principles," says he, " what havock must we make? If we take in hand any volume ; of Divinity, or School Metaphysics, for instance ; let us ask, *Does it contain any abstract reasonings concerning quantity or number?* No. *Does it contain any experimental reasonings concerning matter of fact, or existence?* No. Commit it then to the flames. For it can contain nothing then but sophistry and illusion." P. 259. It is happy for us all, that we are not judges for one another in these cases, but that a wise Providence overrules all things. The *Scriptures* were certainly not meant to come under either of Mr. Hume's characters of *books to be saved from the flames.*

In the preceding observations, I think I have descanted upon every thing of Mr. Hume's, in which it can be pretended, or in which he himself would have pretended, that he had made any advances in the knowledge of the human mind. I need not now say how inconsiderable those advances were. All that he has observed relates to the power of association, and his ideas on that subject were much confined, going very little, if indeed, on the whole, any thing at all, beyond those of Mr. Locke, and others who had preceded him.

Mr. Hume had not even a glimpse of what was at the same time executing by Dr. Hartley, who, in an immense work of wonderful comprehension and accuracy, has demonstrated, that this single principle of *association* is the great law of the human mind, and that all those which Mr.

Hume, as well as others, had considered as *independent faculties*, are merely different *cases* or *modifications* of it; that *memory, imagination, judgment,* the *will,* and the *passions*, have the same, and no other origin ; so that by means of this one property, and the circumstances in which we are placed, we all of us come to be every thing that we are.

In his *Inquiry concerning the Principles of Morals*, Mr. Hume very well illustrates what I fancy he himself would not pretend to be *new*, though, I believe, it had not been sufficiently attended to by metaphysicians, viz. that " utility is the foundation of virtue ;" and this being the most considerable and the most elaborate work of Mr. Hume's, I have referred to it as a specimen of analytical reasoning, in my *Lectures on Criticism.* But in this work Mr. Hume refers the pleasing *feelings*, annexed to the perception of virtue, to *an instinct of nature*, confessedly unable to trace them any farther. " It is needless," he says, " to push our researches so far as to ask why we have humanity, or a fellow-feeling with others. It is sufficient that this is experienced to be a principle in human nature. We must stop somewhere in our examination of causes, and there are in every science some general principles beyond which we cannot hope to find any principle more general." P. 85. Dr. Hartley, however, not resting where Mr. Hume did, has, with wonderful sagacity, discovered the origin of benevolence, of the moral sense, and of every other principle before thought to be *instinctive,* shewing how they are derived from association, affecting us in our infant state, and as we advance in life ; and he has shewn the diversity that we find in human affections to arise from a diversity of influences, operating on us in the same general manner.

In this work, Mr. Hume classes *humility* among the *vices,* with no other view, that I can perceive, but to shew his contempt for the christian system, in which it makes a principal figure as a virtue. And he has wholly overlooked all the virtues of the *devotional kind,* when, in fact, they may be shewn, by arguments independent of the peculiar doctrines of revelation, to be, in their own nature, the most truly *valuable,* as well as the most *sublime* of all others, and to form what may be called the *key-stone* of every truly great and heroic character. Without the virtues of this class (though Dr. Smith considers Mr. Hume as " approaching as nearly to the idea of a perfectly wise and virtuous man as perhaps the nature of human frailty will permit" *), his character must have been as imperfect as his views (looking to nothing beyond the grave) were narrow.

I have thus given you my reasons, as briefly as I well could, for placing Mr. Hume so low as I do in the class of *metaphysical writers*, or *moral philosophers*. As to *Natural Philosophy*, or *Mathematics*, I never heard that he had any pretensions to merit; and of that which constitutes an *historian*, you will not, I imagine, think that much remains to him, besides that of a *pleasing compiler*, after reading Dr. Towers's judicious *Observations* on his *History of England*.† His *Miscellaneous* and *Political* Essays always pleased me, but they by no means entitle him to the *first rank* among writers of either class. As to his *style*, notwithstanding its excellence in some respects, I have shewn in my *English Grammar* (and, as I have been informed, to Mr. Hume's own satisfaction) ‡ that he has departed farther from the true idiom of the English language, than perhaps any other writer of note in the present age.

Submitting all my observations to your own judgment, and sincerely wishing the happiest issue to your laudable pursuit of truth, I remain,

Dear Sir,

Your very humble Servant,

J. PRIESTLEY.

Calne, *March*, 1780.

---

* Conclusion of Adam Smith's Letter annexed to Hume's Life. See p. 325. " In support of this high encomium no proper evidence has ever been produced. Of Mr. Hume's fortitude in adversity, of great generosity displayed by him, or of any uncommon benevolence, no instances are recorded; but these virtues have been eminently and illustriously conspicuous in many Christian characters If the character of *David Hume* be compared with that of *Bernard Gilpin*, a country clergyman, or with that of *Thomas Firmin*, a tradesman of London, but both acting under the influence of the great truths of Christianity, the striking inferiority of this celebrated sceptic will be apparent to every impartial man. But these men were formed by the sublime views of Christianity; and such men were never produced by scepticism or infidelity." *Essay* on Johnson's Life, 1786, in Tracts, 1796, III. pp. 417, 418, by *Joseph Towers*, LL.D. He died in 1799, after having maintained through life, a christian and truly independent character. Dr. Towers's ardour, in advocating the great interests of mankind, I have often witnessed.

† First published, 1778. See Dr. Towers's *Tracts*, 1796, I. p. 283.

‡ " He acknowledged it to Mr. Griffith, the bookseller." Mr. J. Priestley's Note to the *Memoirs*. See also Mr. Tytler's Strictures on the Style of Hume's Essays, in Mem. of Lord Kames, 8vo. I. pp. 236, 237.

Titles in This Series

1: Beattie, James. AN ESSAY ON THE NATURE AND IMMUTABILITY OF TRUTH. 1770.

2: Brown, Thomas. OBSERVATIONS ON THE NATURE AND TENDENCY OF THE DOCTRINE OF MR. HUME, CONCERNING THE RELATION OF CAUSE AND EFFECT. 2nd ed. 1806.

3: Burton, John Hill. LIFE AND CORRESPONDENCE OF DAVID HUME. 1846.

4: Campbell, George. A DISSERTATION ON MIRACLES. 1762.

5: Graham, Henry Grey. SCOTTISH MEN OF LETTERS IN THE EIGHTEENTH CENTURY. 1908.

6: Greig, J.Y.T. DAVID HUME. 1931.

7: Hendel, Charles W. STUDIES IN THE PHILOSOPHY OF DAVID HUME. 2nd ed. 1963.

8: Home, Henry, Lord Kames. ESSAYS ON THE PRINCIPLES OF MORALITY AND NATURAL RELIGION. 1751.

9: Hume, David. THE LETTERS OF DAVID HUME. Edited by J.Y.T. Greig. 1932.

10: Hume, David. NEW LETTERS OF DAVID HUME. Edited by Raymond Klibansky and Ernest C. Mossner. 1954.

11: Jacobi, Friedrich Heinrich. DAVID HUME ÜBER DEN GLAUBEN, ODER IDEALISMUS UND REALISMUS. Ein Gespräch. 1787.
with
———. VORREDE, ZUGLEICH EINLEITUNG IN DES VERFASSERS SÄMMTLICHE PHILOSOPHISCHE SCHRIFTEN. 1815.

12: Jessop, T. E. A BIBLIOGRAPHY OF DAVID HUME AND OF SCOTTISH PHILOSOPHY FROM FRANCES HUTCHESON TO LORD BALFOUR. 1938.

13: Kemp Smith, Norman. THE PHILOSOPHY OF DAVID HUME. 1941.

14: Kuypers, Mary Shaw. STUDIES IN THE EIGHTEENTH CENTURY BACKGROUND OF HUME'S EMPIRICISM. 1930.

15: Laird, John. HUME'S PHILOSOPHY OF HUMAN NATURE. 1932.

16: Priestley, Joseph. LETTERS TO A PHILOSOPHICAL UNBELIEVER. Part I. 1817.

17: Salmon, C. V. THE CENTRAL PROBLEM OF DAVID HUME'S PHILOSOPHY. 1929.

18: Seth, Andrew. SCOTTISH PHILOSOPHY. 1890.